Memoirs of a Pet Therapist

ALSO BY THE AUTHOR

How to Get Your Dog to Do What You Want*
How to Get Your Cat to Do What You Want*

*Published by Fawcett Books

MEMOIRS

of a

PET THERAPIST

▼

WARREN ECKSTEIN

WITH DENISE MADDEN

FAWCETT COLUMBINE

The Ballantine Publishing Group · New York

LIBRARY OF CONGRESS CATALOGING-IN-PUBLICATION DATA
Eckstein, Warren.
Memoirs of a pet therapist / Warren Eckstein.—1st ed.
p.   cm.
"A Fawcett Columbine book"—T.p. verso.
ISBN 0-449-91123-3
1. Eckstein, Warren.   2. Dog trainers—United States—Biography.
3. Animal behavior therapists—United States—Biography.   I. Title.
SF422.82.E34A3   1998
636.089'689'0092—dc21
[B]   97-53125

Manufactured in the United States of America
Text design by Mary A. Wirth

First Edition: September 1998
10   9   8   7   6   5   4   3   2   1

To my parents, Ruth and Charles Eckstein, who kept me from being committed at an early age

To Fay, who believed in me from the beginning

To Denise, who completed the circle

Contents

Acknowledgments

Thanks to Elisa Wares, senior editor, Ballantine Books. Your dedication always puts you at the top of my list. With your incredible sense of curiosity and enthusiasm, you inspired me to dig in and give you *more!*

The exceptional people who have opened their hearts and homes by adopting thousands of homeless cats and dogs I've brought on the various TV shows.

The thousands of people who bring in their pets and animals

to "star" on the various television shows including "Live with Regis & Kathie Lee," "Weekend Today in New York," "The Weekend Today Show," and News 12 on Long Island.

WOR Radio: Rick Buckley, Joe Bilotta, Bob Bruno, David Bernstein, John Gambling, Noah Fleischman; KABC Radio: Bill Sommers, Dave Cooke; WNBC-TV: Kim Gerbasi, Joel Goldberg; "Weekend Today": Beth Ameen.

Dr. Alan Ahearne, Bide-A-Wee, Dan Bleier, Scott Brown, Bruno Cohen, Steve Clements, Diane and Warren DiCarlo, Sharon Graner and The Kennel Club at LAX, Kimberley Conrad Hefner, Jose Monreal, Richard Rosenzweig, Playboy Enterprises, Santa Monica Public Library, Heather Smith, Joanne Udell.

"Seed Money" donors for the Hugs & Kisses Animal Fund: George Shapiro, Howard West; Linda and Alan Hahn on behalf of the Zachary Hahn Foundation; Lynda and Sam Oshin on behalf of the Oshin Family Foundation; Drew Herron, Nancy and Thomas Walsh and Oakley.

I would like to thank my four-footed "models": American paint horse, Apollo Tom; bearded dragon, Lewis; green wing macaw, Jasper; generic cat, Misty; full Chilean Appaloosa llama, M. W. Concho; English bulldog, Oscar; Old English sheepdog, Chelsea; and Christy's Critters pygmy goat, Splish Splash.

And special hugs & kisses to my volunteer "animal wranglers": Rebecca Lowe and Whispering Winds Ranch; Paula and Lewis Turner of the PetCare Company; Heather Crossley; Maria Sanchez, Kristin Campbell, and Christy's Critters.

Preface

Over the years I've adopted out literally thousands and thousands of dogs and cats through my appearances on television and radio. These are pets who were once abused and now are forever loved, and "old-timers" who would have lingered in shelters until their lonely death if it hadn't been for the exceptional people who rescued them. Everyone knows that the easiest pets to adopt out are the very young—puppies and kittens. But as dogs reach the year-old-and-over mark, it starts to be much more difficult to find them a home, and if they have health problems, it's even worse. One of these "special needs" dogs was named Tripod, an eleven-year-old collie who was blind, deaf, and missing a leg. While explaining on a local cable TV show the concept of how I believe animals adopted from a humane society pay you back every day, I told the sad story of how Tripod's owners had died and no one wanted him. It would take just the right kind of person to make sure this dog would be taken care of, considering the commitment involved. This was a dog that maybe had a year or so to live, and with all his disabilities, his care required a high level of responsibility. Now where does one find the right type of person? I don't know if they're sent by God or if their hearts are simply full of love for any living thing, but sure enough, a number of them called for Tripod and he had the chance to spend his last years in love and security. So anytime I lose faith in society or start to feel that people just don't have the feelings of compassion they used to have, I remember the story of Tripod. It always lets me know just how many good people are out there.

Then there was the eighteen-year-old cat whose owners had died and the family was going to have the cat put to sleep because they didn't want to be bothered taking care of it. I mean, what a legacy—this guy obviously adored this cat, pampered it for eighteen years, and now the family wanted to kill the cat because *they* didn't want the responsibility. How does one find a home for an eighteen-year-old cat, which is beyond its years anyway? It amazes me, but we did find a home for her. Over the years, there have been many hard-luck cases and pets who have been mistreated by their owners. And yet, although it is difficult for us to understand why, these blessed creatures are still forgiving. Many people say that's why I'm close to animals, because I don't have that much faith in mankind. Fortunately, there are thousands of people across this country who are unsung heroes, rescuing animals and spreading the message of spaying and neutering. And they restore my belief that man is kind.

I remember some of the battles I had when people would say to me, "Oh, it's just a bad dog," or "It's just a bad cat. What good is it?" I've had this argument with veterinarians and trainers— everyone was an expert. "It has to be put to sleep, or sent away somewhere."

Maybe my way of thinking is a little eccentric—heaven forbid I should ever be called eccentric—but I honestly believe that there are no bad pets, only pets who have been dealt a bad hand by the people they live with.

This is my attitude. Never say never, because there is always something that can be done rather than jeopardize the life or cause any type of pain or injury to an animal.

I believe I was put here to help bridge the gap between people and animals. My ability to "talk" with animals is a lot different from most people. For me, it's simply a matter of understanding that a dog doesn't have to talk like I do. It's understanding an animal's parapsychology or body language. So I get down on the floor with them and speak their language. Sometimes I feel there are thoughts going back and forth between my mind and the dog or cat's mind, like telepathy.

The Amazing Kreskin once said, "Warren, you have an uncanny ability to communicate with animals." And it doesn't matter what kind of animal it is, a snake, a dog, a bird—it makes no difference. We talk to each other. Sometimes I'll see someone walking down the street with a little dog, and instinctively, I'll bend down and give the dog a kiss. There's no facade with animals; if they like you, they'll let you know. They are up front about how they feel. With people, you can meet them for a friendly drink, but then, after you leave, they'll call you an S.O.B. With an animal, you don't get the drink, just total honesty. When I work with animals, we become personal friends. I feel close to them. I'm color-blind, so I have a very strong sixth sense. I'm very instinctive, and my instinct tells me that I've chosen my life's work well.

I've worn out close to a thousand pairs of jeans over the last twenty-five years trying to see the world from a dog's point of view. For instance, I see no reason why owners should try to maintain strict control over an animal at all times. Why does my dog have to walk on my left side (heeling)? It makes no sense at all. How much fun is it for your dog to have to walk in the same position around the block? Let him lift his leg, smell around. Most people are too domineering and bossy over their pets. People need to get rid of their human egos and accept animals more as equals to better understand them. I have seen my dogs laugh at me when I did something stupid. I have seen them yawn when they were bored and smile when they were happy. Try to see the world from your pet's point of view, and act accordingly. You and he will both be happier.

Whether I'm working in Beverly Hills, on Park Avenue, or in

Everytown, U.S.A., one thing is perfectly clear: The value of a pet in the home is worth a million dollars. Money can't bring happiness, but four paws, a wagging tail, and a cold nose certainly can! And remember, always have praise (not food) in your pocket for your pet!

Memoirs of a Pet Therapist

PERSONAL STUFF

Looks Like Muskrat Love

I guess you could say I always wanted to be close to animals, or I always had my hands and feet in poop—any way you want to describe it.

My mother was the Brownie leader for my older sister Nona's troop. On one occasion, when I was about six years old, my mother was escorting two Brownie troops to a park that had a beautiful duck pond. There had to be more duck poop than actual water, but it was just one of those places where kids could go and feed the ducks. I guess I must've just watched Davy Crockett on television, because my parents had bought me the entire "King of the Wild Frontier" outfit. Let me tell you, when you put on the Davy Crockett outfit, you are not the same person. I don't care who you are, after you put on that coonskin hat, you are someone else. I became the mountaineer that Davy Crockett was. I was pretty cool, too, going to a park with all the cute Brownies. I was all dressed up

My sister Nona and myself. Note the snappy animal print.

and wanted to impress the girls by showing them how to feed the ducks and get the ducks to come to them.

Well, while I was feeding the ducks, I slipped on some duck shit, and yes, little Warren Crockett fell into the duck pond. I was covered from head to toe with duck poop. I stunk, *reeked* . . . and painfully, to this day, I can still visualize it. I was beet red, walking out of that pond with my coonskin cap and my pants with the fringes on the sides and matching fringed shirt, covered with duck poop. That was probably one of the most embarrassing moments of my life.

Though I was born in the wilds of the Bronx, I had a natural love for animals. I was an ugly kid and very shy. Our first home was in the Veterans housing project in a rough section of Rockaway Beach, New York. When I was six years old, I was nearly burned at the stake by a gang of neighborhood toughs. They actually tied me to a tree in the swamps, put brush around the tree by my feet, and set it afire. Luckily my friend Richie ran and got help, and other than a few singed hairs, I survived. To this day I don't know why it happened!

When I was in the third grade, our family realized the 1950s dream and moved to a home in a suburb of New York called Oceanside, to a glamorous-sounding street named Bayside Avenue. I grew up in a religiously mixed neighborhood whose households were economically diverse. There were the very poor, called clamdiggers; the hardcore blue-collar workers; and the upper middle class whose fathers were lawyers and businessmen, many of whom were in the garment business. Many of the Jewish kids I knew were in the upper-middle-class families and I was not accepted easily; so most of my friends were very blue-collar and I was the only Jew hanging out with all the Italian and the Irish kids. I took a lot of ribbing for being Jewish, so at an early age—after many beatings—I learned how to fight. Not that my father encouraged it, but he was my hero and never took any crap from anybody. I believed real men had to be tough, and while I was not much of a reader, I devoured everything I could on Wild Bill Hickok, Kit Carson, and Wyatt Earp.

Our house was located on a bird sanctuary called Powell Creek, owned by the U.S. Army. That creek was a great escape for me. And while in forty years I never saw any army people, I did see plenty of mallard ducks, Canada geese, garter snakes, snapping turtles, muskrats, regular rats, and a variety of other critters that my parents were thrilled about me spending my time with. I was one of the proverbial little kids who always brought whatever animals were out there into the house; it didn't matter to me whether it was a field mouse, a lizard, or a snake. One day I brought a rat home and my mother and father looked at me, and with their eyes rolling back said, "What are you going to do with that rat?" I answered, "Mom, Dad, you don't understand: This only looks like a rat; it's really one of those adorable little muskrats. Something is wrong with it—it's lost its hair." And my mother and father just looked at each other and knew that saying "no" at this point was useless. So I kept him and named him "Chas" after my father, who signed his named that way. Naming a rat after your father ... I guess my father didn't appreciate that too much.

I kept Chas for about four or five months. Rats are incredibly smart animals; they make super pets and I'm on the bandwagon for them constantly. People don't understand how smart they are, but I honestly believe that if rats had hair on their tails, they would be incredibly popular pets. It's just their bald tails that scare people off. Anyway, I remember the rat just kept staying like a rat and never grew a muskrat coat of hair. My mother and father kept quizzing me, "How is Chas doing? When is he going to grow his hair back? When are you going to release him back?" Ultimately, I had to release him, but I did have them convinced for a good six months that I had a bald muskrat when it was nothing more than an average, good old-fashioned backyard hangout rat! I let Chas loose, but interestingly enough, the rat maintained a relationship with me. I used to hang out by a drainage ditch behind the house, and for months after I released him, Chas would be there in the afternoon when I came home from school. Then one day he disappeared. Somehow Chas and I bonded and I have fond memories of him.

Charlie

My father bought an auto body shop in Farmingdale, Long Island, called McLean's Auto Body. He never bothered to change the shop's name; so my father, a Jewish guy, owned a body shop with an Irish name. (And people wonder why I travel to the beat of a different drum.)

As soon as the shop opened I decided that he needed a guard dog. I accompanied my father to the local pound where he looked at German shepherds and Dobermans, but I talked him into a mournful-looking, one-hundred-pound Saint Bernard. He had such sad eyes and I immediately called him Charlie, my father's name. How could he say no?

"Where are we going to keep the dog?" I asked my father when we got back to the shop.

"In my office," he replied.

I protested. "Dad, the office is way too small. We're going to need to build Charlie a doghouse."

Well, the doghouse turned out to be quite a project. It was closer in size to a garage than any little doghouse. In the days ahead, this was where I would spend my time—sanding cars and sleeping with Charlie.

I recall driving home that first night and my father bragging, "No one would dare break into the shop with good ole Charlie around." Boy, was he in for a surprise. The next morning, one of the employees called from the pay phone next to the shop. My dad asked, "What the hell's the commotion, Gus?"

"We can't open the shop because this damn *dog* won't let us in!" Gus muttered.

Charlie turned out to be the perfect watchdog. He watched everyone, but the only people he would bark at were the people who worked there. Charlie was the first in a succession of junkyard dogs that I would turn into lapdogs. Needless to say, my dad's shop was robbed regularly; usually with a note that read: "What a nice dog!"

We were so naive that when we decided to get our first at-home dog, my father took me to Macy's. Yes, Macy's had a pet department and they sold dogs. We could not make up our minds whether we wanted a collie or a German shepherd. It was called the Lassie or Rin Tin Tin syndrome in those days. I always felt Rin Tin Tin was more macho, even though *he* was a *she*—pretty risqué for those days! My German shepherd, which I named Smokey, became my best friend. In fact, I still have her first collar. It was also at this time that I would start to spend entire afternoons with the wildlife in my backyard. An afternoon with a snapping turtle was less stressful than an afternoon in the house.

If you grew up in my family, you would probably feel as compatible with the animals as I did. You've heard the story of the relative who came to the bar mitzvah and never left? Along with my new childhood home in this suburban oasis came wall-to-wall relatives. Not only did my mother keep setting an ever-expanding table, but entire new wings of the house kept popping up!

The house was always full of people—relatives, friends—constantly coming and ... staying. When I was in the fifth grade, the first relative to join us was my cousin Joanne, who came to live with us after both of her parents died. When I was a teenager, my mother's parents, Louie and Molly Weiss, retired from the Bronx to their retirement villa on ... Oceanside's Bayside Avenue! Then, after my father's mother passed away, Louie Eckstein joined us. Since Papa Louie was a double amputee, our split-level ranch house had to be made wheelchair-accessible, so my parents took the dining room, cut it in half, and enclosed it as his bedroom and bath.

My maternal grandparents had emigrated from Romania and Austria, so the language difference resulted in my new name, Vadden. I would spend hours on end listening to Grandma Molly tell stories of her childhood in Romania (I guess that's where I get my gypsy instincts). The one that has always stuck out in my mind was the harrowing tale of the white horse.

It was a rainy, early morning in the little town of Falticeni, where Grandma grew up. Just before dawn, Molly would normally be rubbing the sleep from her eyes before starting the long list of chores at the family's farm. Suddenly she heard screams in the distance; then horses' hooves pounding the dirt, galloping closer and closer. A kaleidoscope of terror began to unfold. It was a band of Nazi sympathizers, raiding and ravaging the gentle way of life that Molly and generations before her had revered. The band's speed and stealthiness had enabled them to attack and rape the town's women after swiftly killing the men, including my great-grandfather. It was a horrific experience for a twelve-year-old to comprehend. As they sought Molly next, she ran out to the barn where her family had a white horse. In her own broken words, this was the most incredible horse that ever lived.

The horse maneuvered itself between young Molly and these anti-Semite bastards, and when they tried to accost her, the horse reared up and kicked, giving her the opportunity to run and hide, which ultimately saved her life. I must have heard this story a thousand times growing up.

My grandma Molly suffered a stroke at seventy-two, and it was so heartbreaking watching her try to fight back. I remember sitting with her one day and asking her again about this white horse that saved her life. It brought a smile to her face—the only response she could give. My grandma Molly died shortly after that, but the story of the white horse is in my heart forever! Maybe it's partially the horse saving my grandma's life that made me devote my life to helping as many animals as I can.

The Bickersons

My family's way of talking to one another was to bicker! Not that there was anything wrong with that. All it would take to start an argument in my house was for my father to say he liked the

Mom and Pop leaving on a cruise. Home Alone! I'm sure I managed to get into some trouble!

Brooklyn Dodgers; my grandfather would immediately taunt him by saying that the New York Giants were a much better team. Even the strength of the morning coffee could trigger bickering. I remember my father saying to my grandfather, "I could pee darker than that coffee!"

With over 325 years of life spanning the various family members, it was inevitable that there would be just as many different ways of looking at things! They all loved each other; the bickering was simply their way of communicating. I recall how my grandfathers would argue every weekend as to which was a better car: a Pontiac or a Chevrolet. The wars over which television show to watch were legendary, and there was always a scramble for the best seat in the house.

Privacy was out of the question; just bring up any normal family problem . . . and *pow!!* Everyone became involved, jumping in with a different opinion, and it went round and round that way for hours. It was this constant stress that drove me to escape by spending time with the animals.

I had human friends, but I always felt more at home with animals. They didn't care if my nails were dirty or if I got a D on my report card—and there were a lot of those! I tried to tell the disappointed family clan that if the animals didn't care, why should they? I guess they didn't get it.

Time moves on and so did I. I went on to high school, which was one of my most difficult times. I was shy, bored, and rebellious—what a combination. I was always in trouble. I think my mom spent more time at my school than I did. It was at this point that I began to realize that my mind was more comfortable with abstract thoughts than with black and white statistics. My parents and teachers thought I was lazy and lacked focus, but I knew I was just looking for direction. They even sent me to the school psychologist, who agreed with many of my teachers: I would never amount to anything unless I did it their way. But I was rebellious, and this was just one more reason to rebel.

Smokin'!

As I've said, ours was not a tranquil household, and I grew up banging on the table with knives and forks while my father yelled at me. Someone suggested drum lessons, which I think became my way of letting out my frustration. I'm not a very assertive person, with a tendency to keep a lot inside. Maybe playing the drums was my way of banging it out. As shy as I was, I just loved being in front of a crowd playing the drums, sitting in with little local bands for high school dances and parties. One of the bands I was involved with was a group called the Long Island Sounds—what an incredible name we thought, back then. The band consisted of lead, rhythm, and bass guitar; an organ; drums; and a lead singer. We were all in DeMolay (a younger version of the Masonic Temple) at that point so we played for a lot of their functions.

Wayne, the lead singer of the group, and I never got along. He had dropped out of high school, really thought of himself as a tough guy, and used to be the bully of this group of kids we hung around with. The day I met him we were at a softball game, and Wayne challenged me, "Let's wrestle." I'd been wrestling since I was a kid, watching it on TV all the time, when Rocco and Bruno

Sanmartino were in the ring. So we wrestled and when I pinned him down he split his pants. He was really upset, and it was always tense after that. Wayne's mother worked for RCA Records and actually arranged for the group to do an audition tape for their label. The next day (and I'm sure there was no response that quickly from RCA!), Wayne blurted out, "They loved the band, except they think the drummer really *sucked*." I think that was the last time I spoke to him, and we were later officially turned down.

I had some friends who played in the Fire Department Band for the Oceanside Volunteer Fire Department. That really appealed to me, because as a band member, you could go to the parades and the drills and hang out with the fire guys. We'd march, then go to the block parties afterward. I really enjoyed it and it gave me a sense of belonging. Back then, it was very unusual for a Jew to be in the Fire Department; out of maybe three hundred members, there weren't more than two or three. Now, in my adolescent struggle to be recognized, I was a member of an organization. Fire guys were respected. They were considered tough, drinking, macho-type guys who would go in and fight fires—even though it was a volunteer department. I loved to hang out at the fire house, sneaking a beer now and then, keeping up with the older guys.

The day I turned eighteen, while still in high school, I became an active member of the Volunteer Fire Department Rescue Squad, Number One, in Oceanside, Long Island. It also gave me the opportunity to wear a uniform and carry a badge, which I'd been looking forward to for months! Back then the mascot of Rescue One was Donald Duck, and I had a decal on the side of my car with Donald Duck in a fireman's hat, carrying a first-aid kit, going off to rescue someone.

Once I joined I found out there was a lot more involved than just standing there holding a hose. At Fire School I learned all types of advanced first aid, taking the first EMT (emergency medical technician) course ever given on Long Island; in fact, I still have the card. I would love to sit here and say that what motivated me was my passion to save people, but I think it was more the camaraderie. I always had a fear of being "white collar," and this gave me the chance to hang out with the blue-collar guys and have a beer on a Sunday morning while they washed the fire trucks. I also enjoyed the fact that they loved animals.

As an ambulance technician, I was also the designated driver. Our calls ranged from decapitations at the scene of a car accident to heart attacks and broken bones. I'd lived in this town my entire life, and many of the people I came into contact with were people I knew from the local hardware store or the neighborhood candy store, so it was fascinating. I felt good about what I was doing, but there were also times when it was too personal.

I remember one time being dispatched to a car accident in front of Nathan's, not the Nathan's Famous in Coney Island, but a second one they opened in Oceanside. It was late at night and the victim was someone I had known all through my school years, from grade school to high school graduation. It was a severe car accident and he was partially decapitated; the rest of his body was mangled in a mass of twisted metal. It was one of the toughest calls I had ever gone on.

Part of our job was to rescue firemen in the event of injury, so we would be the first ones behind them during a fire, to help any firefighter who needed to be rescued. And at many fire scenes I had arguments with the guys because after we'd gone in on a search and not found anyone, I'd plead, "Wait, let's go back and bring out the fish" (or the bird or cat or dog or gerbil or hamster). It only takes a little smoke to hurt a parrot. They would shake their heads and mutter, "You're crazy," but I would go back into the fire, because to me, the animals were living things and it was equally important to get them out. I remember, for example, actually stealing an ambulance with my friend Joe Chelluk (who has since passed away), who was also a lover of cats and dogs. At the scene of the fire we found a dog that had been burned and had stopped breathing. I cradled it in my arms and we raced to a local veterinary hospital with Joe driving, the siren going, and me giving mouth-to-snout resuscitation. Taking an ambulance from the scene of a fire and going to an animal hospital . . . let's just say the department wasn't too thrilled about it.

Rescuing animals was just something I did instinctively. And on several occasions I was on the receiving end of a good talking to by the Chief—for using an oxygen mask on a dog or pumping some oxygen into the water of a fish tank. It was kind of a running joke at the fire house; anytime anything involved animals, it was "Let's get Warren involved!" The animals usually recovered well on these occasions, so who cares about a little reprimand every now and then. I mean, these were just things that I would do, and the interesting part about it was that I would start seeing the other guys in the Volunteer Fire Department taking an interest in what I was doing. It was an incredible group of guys, and while they loved to party, they knew what they were there for. They did the job they had to do, and it was a very dangerous one. I broke my shoulder one time by falling off the back of a truck.

One perilous incident took place when I was the first fireman at the scene of a fire. (Because it was a volunteer department, in the event of an actual fire we had the option of going to the fire house and hopping on a truck or using the flashing blue lights on our cars and going directly to the scene of the accident, fire, or whatever the emergency might be.) Anyway, I went in having what they call a Scott Pack or an Air Pack on my back, and I started checking around to make sure no one was in the location. I remember getting really woozy and crawling on my hands and knees until I was totally disoriented and lost. I had no idea which way to go; the smoke kept rolling in thick and black and I just kept crawling around, lost; I knew I was going to die. I thought, "This is it." Then, all of a sudden, I saw a little ray of light and stuck my finger there. My friend and fellow fireman Joe Chelluk swooped in and pulled me out, gave me oxygen, and rushed me over to South Nassau Community Hospital. I believe I spent a week with severe smoke inhalation and some other problems.

Perhaps if I hadn't ended up working with animals, I would have ultimately chosen some type of fire or rescue work. The fire house was a real man's place; every Sunday afternoon there was a poker game going on. I actually remember seeing a man lose the deed to his house at a poker game at the fire house. The men were a fascinating collection of human beings. As volunteers, there was no class distinction. We even had guys who worked at the Fire

Department in New York City as paid firemen and did the volunteer thing during their free time, that's how much they loved it. There were guys who were always getting into fights, guys who were always cheating on this one, or cheating on that one. The majority of them were in their thirties, blue-collar workers, and very patriotic. A lot of them were veterans of the Korean War, or were back from serving their time in Vietnam. Even those who hadn't been in the military had a tendency to be very patriotic. At the time, my hair was relatively long, and they would always make fun of me at the fire house, calling me a "hippy bastard, pinko commie," all those things. They were joking with me, but it was also the way they thought. I remember going to parades with the Volunteer Fire Department and getting into fights because the F. D. guys would say something about the "longhairs" and the longhairs would respond—it was like something out of a B movie.

But it did give me the opportunity to learn how to adapt. Everything in life, I believe, teaches you something. My firefighting days taught me how to adapt to whatever person I may be with at a given time. This was particularly helpful later on when I went into the military and had to live in close quarters with a lot of different personalities. It was a fascinating time of my life and I look back now with a tremendous amount of pride that I was able to be a volunteer for over five years. Some of these guys are still volunteering. I see them walking around town and say hello whenever I can. They risk their lives every single day for us without being paid a dime, but this is what their life is all about: living in town, being a part of it and giving back what they can. They are the most incredible group of men I have ever met in my life, and they deserve a lot more thanks than they get.

Student Activist

By the skin of my teeth I managed to graduate from high school with the rest of the class of 1967. I despised those years; there wasn't one classmate who rated as a friend or a teacher I could connect with. And here I was at a crossroads; I had to make a very major decision in my life. The majority of my classmates were doing everything they could to get their student deferments to avoid the draft, attending the most obscure colleges higher learning had to offer. Paradoxically, I had very patriotic feelings at this stage of my life. Yet there was a conflicting sense of duty to my parents, who had both made a lot of sacrifices so that I could break out of the blue-collar confines that limited their dreams. I really didn't know what to do. My mother persisted with comments like, "Of course, you want to go to college and be a doctor." What else from a Jewish mom?

However, getting into college at this point—we're talking 1966–67—was not an easy task. Literally everybody and their brother was trying to keep from going into the military. And because I had done so poorly in high school, colleges were not exactly waving their pennants at me! But I tested well on the S.A.T. exams and had a guidance counselor who took a liking to me and saw potential. I'll never forget her: Elaine Rapp.

She saw something (or maybe saw *past* something) in my

aptitude, and in speaking with my mother they located three colleges that would accept me—one, I believe, was in Boone, Iowa; another one was down in the Ozarks; and the third, Ricker College, was in Houlton, Maine. Ricker was a Presbyterian college and I think the total student population was approximately one thousand, give or take. I took a short, scenic ride through and it was a very pretty campus. It was way up in northern Maine, the oldest community in Aroostook County, dating back to 1805. I remember driving into town the first time and seeing the War Memorial in the center of town—it was a large potato. You see, Houlton is in farming country and potatoes are the major crop.

Academic life at Ricker College was curious for me since some of the students at this college were in their thirties and here I was eighteen years old. Except for me, of course, and my potential (!), every loser in the world was attending Ricker College. (Interestingly enough, many years later, just on a goof as I was driving around Mars Hill Mountain, Houlton's ski area, I went back to Ricker College. I found a no-trespassing sign nailed up. The school had closed, I believe, two years after I left.)

So here I was, *hating* this place. Everyone was partying, doing some type of drug or drinking Colt 45, the local beverage of choice. I regularly got into fistfights, one of which resulted in my spending three days in jail after a confrontation with a campus police officer who had made a derogatory remark to a friend of mine.

Anyway, I was thrown in a cell with some Native American migrant workers who were there doing some potato picking. My mother had to scrape together twelve or thirteen hundred dollars and I went on all kinds of double secret probation (like in the movie *Animal House*) at the school. I would come home as many weekends as I could, faking everything from mononucleosis to tonsilitis, trying to get into another school. I used any excuse to get my parents to send me money to fly home on weekends, or I'd hitch home, whatever I had to do. Ricker College didn't allow first-year students to have cars on campus—I never understood that rule.

I tried to ground myself by spending lots of time in the out-lying acreage, being the most incredible woodland area of America. While hiking and walking, I spotted bears and moose, white-tail deer, raccoons, possums, and just an incredible array of wildlife. Remember, this was the late sixties. There I'd be, communing with nature, enjoying being around the animals. As a matter of fact, I struck up a friendship with a girl in Maine whose father managed a kennel, and we would go over there sometimes and just hang out with the dogs. I even did some dog training back then to keep my sanity.

Surprisingly, even though I was partying, I did get substantially good grades at this school, because I was learning things that I had the desire to learn. They were getting into biology, psychology, sociology, things I *applied* myself to learn, whereas in high school I had no yearning to learn what a logarithm was. So, because my marks were good, my mother (through a friend of a friend of a friend at Long Island University) was able to get me a transfer to C.W. Post, the LIU campus in Greenvale, which meant I would be moving back home. I don't know which was worse: Ricker College or living at home with my mother and father. They were great people . . . *who just made me crazy.*

Anyway, I moved back to Long Island and went to C.W. Post College, where I pursued my psychology studies. Yet interestingly enough, at that time I spent every moment I had working at local veterinary hospitals, humane societies, anyone who would give me the opportunity to be around animals. I remember I had a friend who worked down at the racetrack where I would go just to be around the horses. I even hung out at the local pet stores. My fascination was a driving force. I knew somewhere in the back of my head—*animals*. I appreciated them for what they were but didn't know where it was going to take me in terms of a career.

While attending C.W. Post, I was taking some advanced psychology classes, and I remember them doing some research. I believe the research had to do with some hallucinatory drugs on rats, to see what type of reaction they had, for some physiological reason. Looking back on it and having been involved with a lot of humane movements over the years, it was probably just a way, at that time, to get some type of government funding or grant money to do research that was probably redundant and abusive to animals, which it turned out to be.

I remember getting up in class and arguing with my professor by saying, "Listen, why should we inflict a *drug of choice* on animals? In other words, these hallucinatory drugs, like mescaline, are not used medically; they are used primarily by people who want to get high! Why should we subject mice, rats, or any other animal to the abuse of pain of a drug that *we* choose to do? I mean, they all have mothers and fathers and they all have hearts." To me, the reasoning behind their research sounded absolutely ludicrous, and yet they went ahead. The fact that this experimentation and research was taking place triggered me to temporarily leave C.W. Post.

And this was not the only place that I had heard about this. Now I started getting involved with the humane movements, gathering more and more information on the amount of animal abuse actually going on in this country. In terms of animal research, I don't want to sound like an abolitionist here, but the bottom line is, going back to those early days of the seventies, it was very sadistic.

C.W. Post College had an equestrian stable with horseback riding, which was the old summer home of Marjorie Post of the Post Cereal family. Located on the North Shore of Long Island, it was a very exclusive place. Anyway, now I was becoming a student activist involved with humane activities and different animal rights groups, which were very splintered back then. I observed that there were issues that needed to be dealt with. While it was true that the horses were all treated incredibly well, it was disturbing to see large colonies of feral cats running around the equestrian center. Outside the humane community, not many people knew we did this, but in the middle of the night we'd sneak onto the campus, set some humane traps (called Have-a-Heart traps), and capture as many of these cats as we possibly could. The purpose was to spay and neuter them then release them back into the area, figuring they can at least live in a colony without multiplying. I wasn't fond about cats living outdoors, but I could accept the notion if they were unable to breed.

I often wonder what people thought when suddenly the

number of cats at the college started diminishing. Did they find out that their cats were getting spayed and neutered, and wonder how? They were only getting spayed and neutered thanks to one of these mom-and-pop groups taking responsibility, and I give them a tremendous amount of support for their inspirational activism.

Meanwhile, I had a lot of my own problems. I was experimenting with drugs and alcohol, and I knew that, in my state of mind, if I didn't get away I'd fall under their devastating influence, as many of my friends had. I remember sitting in a bar the night I decided to enlist, drinking beer and shooters. I was at Vic's Log Cabin, the local hangout for the Fire Department guys and where I celebrated my first drink. The wall behind the bar was papered with letters from all over Europe and Southeast Asia as well as from around the States, written by GIs who had been in the Fire Department and were now doing their time. I decided that lingering around Oceanside all my life was useless; I had to get away. So it was a combination of patriotism and escapism that made me decide to go into the service. The next morning I enlisted, prior to telling my parents, because I knew they would try everything to talk me out of it. I didn't want to listen, so I enlisted first and told them a day or two later.

Off We Go into the Wild Blue Yonder!

I remember well the morning I left for the service. It was one of those unmistakably hot, humid Long Island days. It was before dawn, and I was walking into the house after being out all night with my friends—kind of a going-away party for me. My mother and father were already up, sitting at the kitchen table, which was the focus room for the family.

They had their coffee and their cigarettes and my mother was teary-eyed, crying the entire time. She still hadn't accepted the fact that I was leaving for the service, since I probably would never have been drafted. "Who is *crazy* enough to enlist in the military with a war going on in Southeast Asia?" were her unspoken words, left hanging in the air. She didn't understand the concept that, one, I wanted to get away, and, two, I wanted to do my part.

She couldn't go with me to the base, and she was just too devastated by the whole thing. We got into my father's red Toronado. I told you my father was in the automobile business, and I'll never forget this car. There was no steering wheel. I know this sounds a little unusual. He was trying this new pulley system, where they had these wheels alongside. Going to the service in a car with no steering wheel—that's typical of my life!

We drove down the Belt Parkway to Fort Hamilton in Brooklyn, which was the point of no return. This is where people from the New York area left for the military. Once I walked into Fort Hamilton I knew immediately it was military time, because within five minutes they had thrust a broom in my hand and had me sweeping. For the next couple of hours they put us through some more testing, then I was on a bus with dozens of other sadsacks headed to JFK Airport to catch a flight to Lackland Air Force Base in San Antonio, Texas. Arriving on the ground, there was no getting away from it. Everyone started yelling orders at me and within eight hours my hair was shaved off and I was wearing olive drab green. I spent roughly seven weeks in basic training, learning all the things a good soldier needs to learn: how to march, the Military Code of Ethics, weapons, and just a whole array of things that would serve me later in life. I remember doing drill practice at 6:00 in the morning while being pelted by hail the size of golf balls. In the afternoon we'd tackle the obstacle course, where it was so hot we had to take salt tablets just to keep going. In fact, I passed out one day and had to be carried off on a stretcher—leave it to me to choose basic training in August in San Antonio, Texas!

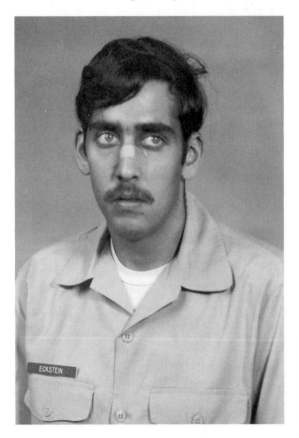

It couldn't have been my big mouth that caused the bruise on my nose! Now you know why I talk to animals.

While I was there, however, I managed to get over to the Air Police Dog Kennels and got real friendly with one of the staff. I spent all my free time working there with him and the dogs until, eventually, it hit me that this was my calling. This is what I wanted to do for the rest of my life!

I entered the service with a bit of an attitude, which got me into a lot of trouble while I was in basic training. I wasn't really good at taking orders, and I guess that played off my sense of humor. We had an intercom system in the barracks that led downstairs, where our sergeant would be, and I remember one time we were all laying in our bunks after lights out. We had done something wrong that day and he had told us all to get on the floor and give him fifty or a hundred, whatever number of push-ups he wanted us to do. Now, my assumption was that he was talking to us from downstairs, over the intercom—there is no way he can see what we are doing—so why should I bother getting down on the floor and doing his push-ups when I can lie in bed and just go "one Sir, two Sir, three Sir, four Sir." Which is exactly what I did! A few minutes later I opened my eyes, and guess who was standing over me? Stripes alive, it was unmistakably the Officer of the Day. I pulled guard duty for the next four weeks after that specific episode.

I got into a lot of disagreements. First of all, I was Jewish, which was not an easy assignment, since there were not a whole lot of Jewish kids in the military at that time, and second of all, I was from New York, which a lot of people didn't like either. So it was kind of a learning curve for me in terms of how to adapt and compensate for the fact that people hated me for a variety of reasons.

After I made it through basic training, I left Lackland Air Force Base and traveled by bus (something ironic about being on a bus in the air force) to Shepherd Air Force Base near Wichita Falls, Texas, which made my college town of Houlton, Maine, look like the hot spot of the world.

I did a lot of escaping acts from there. I remember one time hitching with another GI to Oklahoma City to see the rock band Canned Heat in concert. Being the rebellious soul I was, I wound up befriending a group of Hell's Angels in Oklahoma City. Because of our haircuts it was obvious we were in the military, and luckily a lot of these Hell's Angels were veterans, who kind of took us in under their wing. They brought us to a bar in Oklahoma City where the rest of the Angels hung out—it was a scene I'll never forget. We spent two days there, going AWOL, got back to the base, and ended up in a lot of trouble. While pulling all the extra duty for our escapade, I tried to remember what happened during those two days I spent with the Hell's Angels. All I know is that it must have been a lot of fun!

From Wichita Falls I went overseas to my first assignment with the 601st Direct Air Support Squadron in Germany. Located outside of Frankfurt, Germany, it was a Mobil unit. We both worked and lived out of two-and-a-half-ton trucks, because we had to be ready to roll at a moment's notice. Prior to leaving for Germany, though, I had a thirty-day leave, so I went back to New York, to Oceanside, to say good-bye to my family and friends and kind of break up with the girls I was going out with at that time. I just didn't feel it was fair for me to be in the service while they were there by themselves, and it just seemed that having ties at this point was not the right thing to do. I don't know if I did it more for them or for me. Anyway, I did it.

It turned out that this Mobil outfit afforded me a great deal of freedom, and I spent a lot of TDY (temporary duty) traveling all over the world. While in Europe, I had access to a jeep, along with permission to do pretty much whatever I wanted—so I spent virtually all of my off-duty time driving around Europe, working mainly with the large training kennels. I had the opportunity to handle an amazing variety of animals while being exposed to some incredible European training techniques, such as Schutzhund training, Polizeihund training, and Belgian Ringsport. These people were way ahead of us in terms of training approaches. Their techniques taught dogs to be very obedient against all types of obstacles. Traveling up the Main and Rhine Rivers, I was introduced to some of the European breeds that I would never have gotten to work with had I stayed in the States. Incredible dogs like the Leonberger (which, by the way, I thought was a Jewish accountant when I first heard the name). There was the briard, the Bouvier des Flandres; I got down on my hands and knees with giant schnauzers, Dobermans, Great Danes, German shepherds, and an amazing breed called a hovawart as well as rottweilers in the actual town of Rottweil, Germany.

During my time in Europe I was introduced to many trainers and behaviorists from universities and traveling circuses where I began to work with primates and large cats. There was much to learn from these trainers, and we used to engage in some very heated discussions at the local guest houses (the U.S. equivalent to our local tavern) over much Steinhaeger and beer. I felt that many of the techniques were a little too strong and convinced many that my hugs and kisses approach would work better.

Many times when I got back to the barracks, my fellow GIs would joke because I would be scratched up from working with the exotic animals, and they would think I was out with a wild Fräulein and just used the animals as a cover-up. Believe me, it wasn't a cover-up, it was a lion or a tiger or a bear!

My passion to experience every facet of animal training in Germany would lead me, dangerously, toward the verboten. For months I had been hearing about some incredible trainers on the other side of The Wall—the Berlin Wall in East Germany. However, because I was in the military holding the highest possible clearance—a top-secret crypto clearance with the U.S. government—I was not allowed in any way, shape, or form to cross the border and go to East Germany. I hope the statute of limitations is over, because I did find a way (through my animal friends) to get across the border to East Berlin and meet with some people. I remember they gave me a paper saying that I was a schoolteacher, and I was able to cross over for an introduction to a renowned trainer, a guy who specialized in Schutzhund training. It was just incredible to watch his dogs and his approach. I initially thought of this training as being negative, but the rapport this man, Max, had with his dogs was absolutely amazing. I learned an awful lot in the four or five hours I spent with him. For instance, the concept that if you have a dog that doesn't want to jump a fence, teach it to retrieve a ball. If you have a dog that wants to retrieve a ball, don't teach it to jump a fence. Basically, you take what the dog's natural instinct is, then use it to gain, ultimately, what you want. Don't try to teach the dog something it doesn't want to learn, because it's never really going to be super at it and never going to enjoy doing it. And remember, if you enjoy doing something, you're always going to get a good response, and that holds true for animals. So it was an incredible few hours that I spent in East Germany, but the whole time I was there, I kept looking over my shoulder and thinking, "If I get caught, God am I in trouble. Will I spend time in an East German jail or will the West German government take me and put me in their prison? Will they court-martial me as a spy, or . . ." It was a scary time, but I did make it back to West Germany undetected and continued on with my military service.

Like every kid in the service, I loved getting mail, but boy did I hate writing. I had too many important things to do, too many women, too many guest houses to go to. So I really didn't write much at all, but six thousand miles only enhanced my mother's power to wield the Jewish guilt with letters like this:

Dearest Stinker Warren,

It's not enough that I hear from you so rarely, I have to contend with grandma's big mouth saying you don't love her. Ye god's son, what's happening? Let's hear it, BUB.

I don't know too many of your friends from the Fire Department but strange faces keep coming over to me to ask how you are. Of course I don't tell them I don't have the slightest idea. I did study drama in high school.

Almost a year ago since you left for the Air Force. It

seems like ten years. Be good, be careful, CALL and
WRITE. All my love, Mother. Enclosed is stamp and sta-
tionery money.

Whenever my mother signed anything "Mother," I knew I was
in trouble. I did get to extend my stay in Germany and continue
my studies with the animals. For a couple of weeks I was working
in this really remote area in Germany. It was called the Bonames
Army Air Field, and to this day I still don't know what they did
there. Small planes would fly in and out with some big generals
aboard and some big officers, and we were there to protect the
planes. Anyway, I wasn't one to go downtown much, so the guys
would always bug me, "Come on, Eckstein, we'll have a few Stein-
haegers and maybe meet a couple of Fräuleins." Finally they convinced me and we headed downtown. I remember walking into a
bar and having these beautiful ladies sitting next to me, asking me
to buy them a drink. Boy was I impressed, not realizing at the time
that the cognac and Coke I was paying for was nothing but plain
Coke—costing me five or six dollars a drink. Anyway, it didn't
take me long to catch on to what was going on here—I think it
was six to eight months later, just joking. This bar was right out
of a John Wayne movie. I walked in there with some GIs from
all over the United States and on the jukebox (and I think in
every jukebox in every military area) they had the "Battle Hymn of
the Republic" and "Dixie." When they played the "Battle Hymn,"
all the northerners would stand up. When they played "Dixie," all
the southerners would stand up. It was Civil War déjà vu. I remember fights breaking out with chairs and bottles flying; they were

rough 'n tumble barroom brawls out of a Wild West movie. One time, something broke over my face and I looked like a monkey when I woke up the next morning—it was so swollen. A few stitches later, though, and I was back on my feet. Anyway, the black eye, the stitches, and the swollen lip did not discourage me from going back the next night.

I met a lady there—Ursula, or Ushi, as it became later. We became really friendly; obviously, there was an attraction. Just enough for me to overlook that she was, how can I put this, a bar girl/hooker. In saner moments, a jealous person like me would not even dream of getting caught up in this situation; however, at this point, my mind was so out of focus that it didn't bother me. So I started dating this West German hooker, who, by the way, had been married twice—to two other American GIs in the United States—divorced twice, and was now back living in Germany. She was "the older woman," twelve years my senior, and it became a fantasy setup—I spent a lot of time off base, hanging out at her very expensive apartment in downtown Frankfurt. She bought a brand-new BMW and gave me the keys so I could drive it around wherever I wanted to go. It was a great escape from the stifling reality of the service. While I was with her, I adopted a stray dog—what a shock, right? A little puppy that couldn't have been more than the size of my fist. I named him Cappy and he became my European dog. When I was sent to other places, and finally when I had to return to the States for good, I had to leave the dog with her. It was devastating to me; I mean, that I was really going to miss him—the *dog!* Needless to say, my Jewish mother back in Long Island was not thrilled about my relationship with Ushi. One time I remember getting on the phone, wherever I was, and saying to her, "Ma, I think I'm going to get married," and she shouted to my dad, "Charlie, get me tickets for Pan Am, I'm going to Germany right away!"

When it came time for me to decide whether I wanted to stay in the service or leave, my wandering mind and spirit needed only fifteen seconds to decide that it was time to move on, and so I did. From Germany I was sent to Langley Air Force Base in Virginia, where I spent about five or six months before being discharged. While at Langley I decided to buy a car, and my mom lent me five or six hundred bucks to buy a brand-new 1970 Duster 340, which I still own. (The original bill of sale is still in the glove compartment.) I started driving back to Oceanside every weekend, exhilarated by (almost) having my freedom, as well as by the magnificent scenery along the route through the towns of Virginia, Maryland, and Delaware.

Because it was a hot car, my Duster tended to overlook posted speed signs, and one time when I was driving myself and some buddies through Delaware, we were pulled over by a Delaware state trooper. He took us to the courthouse where we had to appear before a magistrate, or whatever they call them there, who levied a $100 fine. Among the three of us in the car, we had maybe seventy-five cents combined; so here we were at two or three o'clock in the morning, we had to be back on base at six, and we were being threatened with jail because we had no money. When the first sergeant at the base was called at this ridiculous time in the morning, he guaranteed the magistrate that on our next paycheck he would get his money, which he did. It wasn't an isolated incident; because of my hot car and quick temper, I had a tendency to get a lot of tickets. As a matter of fact, there was a time when I went before a judge in Hampton, Virginia, who asked me when I was being discharged from the service. "Two weeks," I answered. His exact words to me were: "If I were you, son, I wouldn't be coming back to Virginia for quite awhile." I just had so many speeding tickets. I wasn't a reckless person, but I think at that time my life was going so fast, that my car just followed. It was probably good that, for many weekends, I couldn't afford to buy gas. So even with the car, I had to hitchhike between Langley in Virginia and New York. Some of the experiences I encountered while hitching were amazing.

During my last days in the service I sank into a deep depression. I can't exactly pinpoint the cause, but I felt very lonely. I knew I didn't belong back on Long Island, going back to the lifestyle I had before enlisting in the service. Yet I didn't know where to go or what to do, and I have to admit that, at this time, my life was at a very low ebb. I can't say I was at the point where I was contemplating suicide, but I was drifting. I had no direction and zero focus.

I remember doing a lot of walking, specifically in a place called Buckaroo Beach, which was ironic because, when I was a kid, my father used to tell me stories of Buckaroo Beach, and he was also stationed at Langley Air Force Base when *he* was in the military. After spending a couple of weeks at the barracks at Langley, a couple of GIs and myself decided to rent a bungalow at Buckaroo Beach. Walking along the jetty that would break the waves right along the beach, I contemplated a final jump into Chesapeake Bay. I mustered up all the faith I had never called on before and appealed to myself, "OK, get on with your life. Things are going to turn good. Focus on what you love most, more than anything else in the world: *animals*."

Love at First Sight

At sixteen I had looked like the punk you've always warned your daughter about. I was a greaser, considered a hood. This wasn't an earned reputation; I wasn't a bad kid. It was my hair—all slicked with VO 5 in that "waterfall" cut that just screamed "he's a rebel."

I was at the Garden City Bowl when our eyes first met, across the glistening alleys. I didn't know it, but Fay Schwartz was twelve years old. I went over to talk with her, but her friends and her older sister drew up a line of defense that did not allow me to approach her. Fay and I saw each other several times after that encounter, but always with her friends and family hovering protectively. So, a few words were all we got to speak.

In 1971, on leave from Langley Air Force Base, my discharge soon to be a reality, I was testing civilian life by tooling around Oceanside in my 1970 Duster with my friend Jay. It was incredible to be back, savoring my freedom. Yet once again, I had to get out of the house! At this point, the number of family members living under the same roof in my childhood home had boosted to an all-time high: fifteen. I claimed the only space left, a corner in the basement—actually the furnace area. To decorate it, I went to Pergament and bought some funky stick-on shag carpet squares to cover the floor, walls, and ceiling. Being color blind, I had no idea what they looked like, but everyone who came in wore sunglasses.

One day as I was driving I saw this raven-haired, willowy figure walking down the street by herself. I honked my horn and waved like I knew her. Just a glimpse of this girl/woman simply dazzled me. Not missing a beat, she stuck her nose in the air and quickened her step.

I circled around the block several times to catch another glimpse of her face. She looked familiar, but I couldn't place her. How could I forget a face like that? She even haunted me that night in my dreams, until I woke up, startled and mumbling. *"She grew up.... It's ... Fay!"*

It took sheer guts to pick up the phone and call her. Remembering all the times I tried to approach her, I wondered if she'd think I was stalking her? Did she have a boyfriend? Probably some North Shore preppie. Maybe she'd joined the antiwar movement and was disgusted by my tour of duty. After calling information for her number—I knew she lived on Emery Street in Hempstead—I took a deep breath and dialed. When she answered, I said, "Hi, Fay, you probably don't remember me ..." Actually, she did, and we talked for nearly an hour. Someone had told her I was in the service, and I learned that she was seventeen and in her senior year of high school. I told her I had six months left to serve in Virginia before completing my service duty, but I'd have a three-day pass the coming week; could I drop by then? She welcomed me back, and so on our first date, when the sky is the limit, Fay Schwartz took advantage of an impoverished serviceman by asking me to take her to dinner—at Jack in the Box.

Naturally, we talked about animals. Just like me, she was addicted to retrieving animals and bringing them home to Mom.

Her mother, Linda, was an Australian war bride who had spent much of her life in the outback. She always whistled at birds and listened for their answer. Her mother always knew when a storm was coming, because the birds would tell her. Fay learned from her mother that if you respect nature, it will take care of you. The language of the animals was something she was taught to appreciate and never take for granted.

I met her family, which included her mother and her older sister/protector, Sharon. Fay's father, who had been an assistant postmaster, had died just a couple years earlier, when Fay was fifteen.

Fay had specific goals in life. She planned to be an attorney, and had scholarship offers from Vassar and St. John's University. But surprisingly, I wasn't intimidated by her academic achievements. She listened encouragingly when I revealed my dream of turning my love for animals into a career—others I had told had merely rolled their eyes. She believed in me not on a "let's pretend" level, but . . . could it be??? Almost like "I want to follow the dream with you." Or was I imagining it?

As independent as she seemed, Fay was very vulnerable. The death of her father probably made me feel especially protective of her. I felt profoundly connected to her in the limited time we shared, and life became lighter when Fay tackled it with her eagerness and humor. Remembering the way my parents loved each other, it hinted of an exciting future.

I was supposed to see Fay over Christmas when I had leave time, so I bought her an immense musical jewelry box at JC Penney in Virginia. I had the Duster, but I had no money for gas or tolls, so

I decided to thumb my way north. I learned an important lesson that night. Never hitchhike on Christmas Eve—people are a little buzzed out!

I was picked up by three drunks who were swaying back and forth all the way from Virginia to just outside Washington, D.C., which included the fourteen-mile drive across the Chesapeake Bay Bridge and Tunnel. It was the scariest ride I ever took in my life, even though I must admit I participated in the passing of the Jack Daniel's bottle around the backseat of the car. They dropped me off in a remote area; I couldn't see a thing, but I heard a lot of barking dogs. The jewelry box doubled as a great seat while I was waiting for cars to come along.

Now, I know you're not going to believe this, but this is a true story. Out of the clear blue on this dirty, dust-ridden road outside Washington, D.C., in Maryland somewhere, I saw a car's headlights in the distance. Moments later, a very attractive young lady stopped the car, picked me up, and drove me back to the main road. I wouldn't have done it, but luckily for me *she* did. What's normally an eight- or nine-hour drive took me well over twenty-four hours to hitch home, in uniform the whole time and schlepping this enormous jewelry box.

Fay continued to see me, but since I wasn't around every day, she also spent time with a long-haired blond musician in her class at school. After stewing over this at Langley, I gave her an ultimatum: I told her that unless she quit seeing him, I would start hanging out with our female counterparts at the base, the WAFs. So she agreed, and I proposed to her before she graduated high school in June.

We started planning a big wedding, but it became too complicated, so we decided to elope. I insisted on some romance, so we hopped into my Duster and headed for Niagara Falls. Near Kingston, I tired out, so we knocked on the proverbial Justice of the Peace's door. He performed the ceremony in front of the fireplace of his home, with his daughter as maid of honor, and me in my wedding suit: bell-bottom jeans, sandals, and an air force fatigue shirt.

As the newlywed couple, we honeymooned overnight at the Holiday Inn Kingston, where Fay, my virgin bride, was so nervous

Posing with Fay and Sir Laurence, a pound refugee turned celebrity.

she spent most of the wedding night in the bathroom reading Archie and Jughead comics.

I Coulda Been a Mailman!

Well, I had just gotten out of the service and taken a bride; now I needed a job. My new mother-in-law was pressuring me to take the civil service test, so she could use her influence to get me hired at the post office in Long Beach, New York, where Fay's late father had been the assistant postmaster. "I can get you into the post office; you can become a mailman with a good income, great benefits, and a civil service career *for your entire life!*"

I had just gotten out of uniform and was very dubious about getting back into one, so I resisted. Besides, there was no longer any doubt: I wanted to work with animals. I knew veterinary medicine was not for me, and neither was grooming. I didn't have the patience to stand in one place all the time, so I looked at the options available. I liked the notion of helping people communicate with their pets, analyzing the behavior of not just the animal but its owner, then solving problems right in the home. Roughly, that was the job description for what I dubbed myself as: a pet psychologist. I had no idea, however, where one could find a job as a pet psychologist; obviously, there were no ads for one in the *New York Times*. After telling our families about my career choice, both my parents and Fay's mother wanted to get *me* into therapy, *fast!*

With my twelve-week unemployment from the service running out, and turning down an offer to sell paint at the local hardware store for three bucks an hour, I took a job behind the counter at a dry-cleaning store. Yes, that was my beginning, a dry-cleaning store. When you work at a dry cleaners, you have customers who come in every other day, every three days, and they bring in clothing that is covered with dog hair, cat hair, or God knows what kind of hair. Anyway, I'd start up a conversation. We would talk about the hair on their clothes and, ultimately, how the pet hair got on their clothes. They started telling me the problems they were having with their pets, and I realized there really was a need for what I wanted to do. Yet I still had no idea how to get that need out to the public. People all had questions: "My cat is peeing on the floor," "My dog is jumping on my mother-in-law," "What do I do? What do I do?"

I turned to my wife at this point and said, "Fay, I really need to grab the attention of these people." So we brainstormed and, investing our last eight dollars, took out an ad in the PennySaver that circulated in the five towns of Long Island—a very affluent area with a high Jewish population. The ad began:

"WE'LL TEACH YOUR DOG YIDDISH FOR $15."

Well, the phones started ringing, and people explained their pet situations. Whether it was housebreaking, jumping, chewing, whatever, I would go into their homes and solve their pets' problems.

Once I started doing that, recommendations followed. It was "networking" before networking had a name. One person would tell another person who would tell another person, and so on. It was the American dream—move to the suburbs, get a pet, have problems, call Warren—it all followed in quite an interesting path. Then they would recommend me to their veterinarians. "Hey, you're not going to believe this! This guy came to my house, and, you know, my dog has been growling for five years. All of a sudden, my dog behaves like Lassie." So things were starting to gel.

What I didn't know was: How does one start a business? You needed a couple hundred dollars to incorporate, and I still had no money. I thought I would work at pet stores around town— basically they would pay in leashes and collars so I could go out and train dogs. During this process I met a really nice lady. I didn't realize she had any problems, and she asked if I would teach her how to train dogs. I said, "Sure, no problem." So I taught her how to train dogs, and she became my partner. Unbeknownst to me, my new partner was a major drug user. I should have trained my drug dogs to sniff *her* out! I would end up working 112 hours a week and she would end up working 6. At the end of the week we would split the seventy-five bucks' profit we made. This lasted for a year or so, until I finally realized it just wasn't working out. I bought her half of the business for like a hundred dollars. And then I started on my own.

At this point, things started to click. Fay and I founded the company, calling it Master Dog Training. I'll never forget that. People said, "What a great name, Master Dog Training!" Remember now, folks, this was the seventies. It could be interpreted as, you could be the master of your dog, or I was a master training your dog.

Business started to snowball and the phones started ringing

off the wall. I knew I wasn't going to be able to handle this all by myself; I was going to have to hire people. My reputation was on the line at this point, and I began saying to myself: "Hiring people is not the answer. Let me find the right people and I'll train them myself." This way, at least, when they went out to work with clients, they would be training the same way I did. Ultimately it got to the point where we were doing so much work that we were training more and more people. At the highlight of the Master Dog Training days, we had fourteen trainers on the road full time. We were seeing somewhere between three and five hundred dogs a week. All this, mind you, while I worked at the YMCA training a couple hundred dogs a week myself. So it was a busy time in my life. One hundred twelve hours a week went to the dogs!

EARLY PET
YEARS

The Barking Parrot

When Fay and I first got married we lived in a building called Riviera Towers, which was populated mostly by retired Jewish couples. We called them the "snowbirds," for they would fly down to Florida for the winter and return to Long Island for the summer. I can still smell the chicken soup and God knows what other Jewish dishes they used to make. We had a studio apartment that was *so compact*, the two of us could barely turn around at the same time. But it was the only place we could afford—at $216 a month. I'll never forget that figure because God did we have to sweat to make those payments.

At first, we did not have any pets. Fay had a dog that was living at home with her mom and I had some pets that were with my mom. We knew that, because of our busy work schedules, we would not have pets for at least a couple of years. Now, this was an era when there was a lot of drug use going on. People were either smoking pot or dropping acid, doing Quaaludes, or taking methamphetamine. Thus, it was common to walk into a house and find the clients using drugs. Some even offered to pay me in drugs. One client whose dog I was training also had a pet bird, and this client really enraged me when he told me that one of his friends had put some LSD in his pet bird's water; the bird had not been the same since. Well, of course, you know what a little bit of that drug can do to humans; imagine how it affected the bird. The poor thing was basically stoned out of its mind. This guy didn't really like the bird anyway, so after some negotiation I took it home to Fay. Now the question was what were we going to do with a wacked-out parrot? You couldn't talk to him, and you couldn't handle him. The only thing the parrot did was bark. It had picked this up from mimicking the former owner's dog, which was why I was originally called in: to solve the chronic barking. So there we were in this little studio apartment, which strictly prohibited dogs and cats, with a barking parrot. Pretty soon I started finding notes that neighbors had slipped under the door saying "Keep your dog quiet." Then one night two Long Beach police officers showed up at my door with the apartment manager, Stu, a crabby man who bellowed, "I told you when you moved in that you could not have a dog. People are complaining. Now I'm here with the police and you are going to have to get rid of it." Happily, I invited them into my apartment and introduced them to my parrot Tattoo who, in fact, barked like a dog. Everyone started to laugh and the police all thought it was a big joke. Nonetheless, we almost lost the apartment over that recovering barking parrot.

Peace Officer Days

Bless the Beasts and the Children,
   for in this world they have no choice, they have no voice.
Bless the Beasts and the Children,
   give them shelter from a storm; keep them safe, keep them warm.

It was the late seventies. Throughout the early years of my career, I found myself helping many humane organizations. If they adopted out a pet that had a problem, I would work with the pet until the problem was resolved—at no charge.

There was one humane group that I really respected. It was a very small group of volunteers, but they worked harder than any other group around.

Fay and I decided to help. We formulated our own chapter and started looking for volunteers. We met monthly and used my office as a base of operations. The organization was very involved in cruelty investigations, and after receiving peace officer status, I was put in charge of a dozen other officers.

Our mission was to enforce little-known, seldom-used state agriculture and marketing laws, designed to provide humane treatment for animals. If someone was found guilty, the maximum sentence was one year in jail and a $500 fine.

We had the power to enforce the act by issuing summonses and making arrests, but we had to buy our own uniforms and guns. I questioned why a gun, but after my first few investigations, it became clear.

Two out of every five complaints involved actual cruelty and ran the gory gamut of pets being locked indoors without sufficient food or water while their owners were on vacations, being beaten with sticks and rubber hoses, plus drownings, hangings, and tortures such as tying firecrackers to an animal and lighting them. The staged dogfights, cockfights, neglect and abuse were especially difficult to handle.

Our group won its first conviction within its first two months in operation, against a Smithtown man charged with neglecting a horse. It was a sickening discovery. The poor animal was covered with blood oozing from flea-bitten ears and open sores. Once majestic, now he could barely use his legs because of overgrown hooves. Can you imagine the frustration that must have bedeviled such a proud creature when he would try to stand and topple over, slamming repeatedly into a cramped stall? His bloated belly, dull coat, and slightly swayed back revealed a deadly state of malnutrition, and what we feared for most was the acute depressed state he was in.

Fortunately, his fate was safe in the hands of a veterinarian skilled enough to gradually return the horse to a healthy state, and he was retired to a farm. The disgusting owner received a sentence of six months' probation.

Because the laws were never really enforced before, our progress in enlightening the public was slow but encouraging. Word started to spread that it was against the law to abandon animals and ignorance was no excuse. A couple of women who worked for an animal clinic witnessed a man throwing a puppy out of a van that had pulled over to the side of the road. They cut off the driver, retrieved the animal, and recorded the van's license plate number. It made my day to issue a summons charging him with abandoning this precious female shepherd mix, just three months old and left to fend for herself. Tails wagged when he ultimately wound up serving jail time.

These crimes were committed by all types of people all over Long Island, from the richest to the poorest. Unbelievably, in August of 1976, when Hurricane Bell hit our region, we got more than fifty calls about dogs tied to trees or posts and left outside without shelter during the entire storm.

I also investigated pet shops with overcrowded, dirty cages and those who employed unqualified help to administer injections and care.

Many of the cases were simple neighbor versus neighbor feuds, but others bordered on the complexity of the French Connection. One perilous time someone had phoned accusing the owners of a motorcycle shop of mistreating a dog. I went into the shop dressed in plain clothes to see for myself what was going on. I started asking questions, and the next thing I knew I was surrounded by at least half a dozen Dennis Hopper look-alikes. These guys didn't put cops on a pedestal to begin with, so you can imagine how I felt when someone yelled, "You're a what? A dog cop?" After they stopped laughing, one of the guys barked at me, "Is that a military tattoo?" Looking to lighten up the moment (and to save my ass) I said "No, just a drunken night in Bangkok." We started to talk and the lines of communication opened. It turned out that it was a nuisance complaint by a neighbor who didn't like the loud sounds or the looks of these Easy Riders. In reality, their bullterrier was actually treated better than a new Harley.

There was a really large park with a reservoir on Long Island called Hempstead Lake State Park. There was also a riding academy on the grounds, from which people could rent horses and go for rides.

For years and years it had been known that a pack of dogs ran wild there. Increasingly, the state park police were receiving reports that the dogs were occasionally harassing people on horseback by biting at the horses' feet and jumping up on them. As a result, the police decided to take matters into their own hands; secretly, a couple of park police officers were going out early in the morning to hunt the stray pack of feral dogs. They killed about half a dozen and buried them, but then somehow the story leaked to the press. People were outraged. How do you take your kids to the park and tell them to respect and obey officers who kill dogs for target practice?

Because I was a peace officer for the state of New York, and because of my background and knowledge in terms of dealing with wild as well as domestic animals, the parkway police called me in to meet with them. They could no longer afford to shoot these dogs, nor should they have in the first place—they needed a better solution.

So I went in and met with the two officers responsible—I swear their names should have been Bubba and Ernest. They were big, beefy-looking guys who just glared at me and said, "You *are* going to do the right thing, *aren't you?*"

It didn't occur to me at that point, but they were presupposing that I would agree with any statements they made to the press, otherwise I would get in trouble. The papers then interviewed me, and I contradicted everything they said.

Through the reporter, I challenged, "Why don't they go into the park with tranquilizers and traps and try to get these animals in a humane way." And that's ultimately what we did. I brought along six volunteers, three of whom worked for me professionally. (During this pursuit, my business shut down for about two weeks.) Every morning at about three or four o'clock, we would venture into the park searching for the pack of stray dogs. There were about six dogs in the pack and the leader was a large shepherd-type dog. He was incredibly beautiful and intelligent. In fact, he outsmarted me for about two weeks, until we were finally able to capture him.

Armed with a tranquilizer gun, this was the closest to hunting I ever wanted to be. For two weeks straight we would head out into the forest before dawn and just sit there. One morning we came along one of the creek beds and I heard a whimpering. My sense of sound is very acute and I figured this might be a lead. We followed the sound, and we found a burrow.

I reached into the burrow, thinking God knows *what* is down there, and some creature nipped at me. I took my bleeding hand out, thought a moment, then reached in again and pulled out a puppy, followed by another puppy, and then one more.

I was fascinated by this: Imagine how many thousands of years dogs have been domesticated. Now, obviously, the dogs in the park started out as domestic animals; perhaps they had never seen people, but they were not wolves. Yet these dogs had reverted back to incredibly instinctive behavior by first digging the burrow along the creek, which is very common. Then there were areas where you could see that the adult dogs had eaten their food and then regurgitated it so the puppies would have something to eat.

We ultimately captured the six adult dogs with either the Have-a-Heart trap or the tranquilizer guns. Some of them were sent to a farm area, but all the dogs found a home.

The puppies, on the other hand, needed special attention. After we pulled them out, the press claimed there was nothing we could do with them and they would have to be killed. When the story broke, we were inundated with calls from people wanting to adopt these now famous "media" pups. Yet finding them a home was not so simple; they all needed a lot of work in the process of socialization. Consequently, I volunteered my time to work with these dogs. In the beginning, they displayed a lot of aggression. It took many months. Understand that, psychologically, a dog grows in a period of twelve months. So even if the puppies were only five, six weeks old, they had already reached the stage of the "terrible twos" of human children and had a good sense of what was going on. The training took a tremendous amount of time before the animals were put up for adoption. Fay and I had fostered them all, so they bonded to me like I was their mother in the wild, and their leaving was a wrenching moment. I know for a fact that the pups turned out to be really great dogs. I still hear from one owner, who just thanked me profusely for the dog because it was such a wonderful match for her and her family.

This same scenario repeated itself, but with stray cats. We would go into the industrial areas of New York and catch feral cats, and with a lot of tender loving care and lots of socializing, they were eventually brought around and could make someone a loving, happy pet. Those people who say "nothing can be done" are simply wrong. When it comes to something that lives and breathes, there is always something one can do. I cannot make them all Morris, and I cannot make them all Rin Tin Tin, but I can make them all livable, lovable, productive members of the family.

It was one of the coldest nights I can remember. Long Island had just been hit with a major snowstorm and power was out all over. I got a call at home from a local police precinct that would generally call me when they had an animal case. A woman notified them that her neighbor was away and had left her dog tied up in the backyard. It was about 10:00 at night when I arrived on the scene. Mind you, this was a well-to-do neighborhood. When I went into the backyard, to my horror and disbelief, I saw an emaciated beagle, tied to a short chain, whose paw was frozen in the ice; he had gnawed at it until it was just about off. I picked him up, put him in a blanket, and drove about twenty miles to a twenty-four-hour veterinary clinic. The vet told me that he would have to amputate the paw immediately and to hope for the best. I paid the veterinary costs out of my own pocket, well over $1,000. The beagle survived the next critical hours, and eventually found his way into a loving and nurturing family. His owner got off with a $50 fine for animal cruelty.

Then there was the case of the Refreshing Springs Church. I received a call that a religious group was sacrificing animals in the basement of the church. The partial remains of goats, lambs, and chickens were seen in the garbage! I arrived at the church on a Friday evening. I entered and was greeted by someone who asked what I wanted. I told him about the complaints I had received and that I wanted to see the basement. He called out, and I was soon being assaulted by several demonic-eyed wild men and pushed out of the church. I was really nervous. That was the only time I exposed my gun, but I know it saved my life. On my CB radio I called for police backup, and when they arrived we went back in. I issued a summons on the spot. However, after months of trying to prosecute the case, it was dropped. In my opinion it was dropped because the case became entangled in the quagmire of the Right to Worship issue, and the group qualified as a religious sect. I believe this kind of sacrifice goes on all over the country.

While neighbors might call to expose the heinous acts in their neighborhood, finding someone willing to testify was the major obstacle we had to contend with in our investigations. Our work was further hindered by little or no cooperation from the police and by the threat of attacks by the animal owners under investigation or by the animals themselves.

My officers and I investigated hundreds of complaints and successfully prosecuted many first-time animal abuse cases. It was a bloody battle to save the pets, who would often lick the hand of the abusers between the blows they would suffer.

THE TRAINING YEARS

When I first starting training, there were only three other companies providing a similar service for dogs and everyone offered a free evaluation of your pet. In other words, someone would come to the client's house and tell her, for example, if the dog was shy, or aggressive, or outgoing. The evaluation was made by giving the equivalent of a doggy IQ test. Based on that, I would then speculate as to how much training I felt was needed to resolve the behavior problems and then quote a price.

Hanging out with Muggs, Shannon, Honey, and Lady, four of my eight strays that saw the vacancy sign out on my upstate farm.

Once I quoted a price, that was the price no matter how long it took. For example, if I said six to eight weeks, and the training took twelve weeks, then I had underestimated the time and I had to eat the difference.

We would do these evaluations free of charge. And because there were other dog-training businesses, clients would get three or four different quotes on the cost of training. The other trainers hated me because I was able to outsell them. Growing up with such a diversified life, I was able to really talk to people. As a result, it made no difference if the client lived on Park Avenue or in Levittown—I could adapt to whomever I was speaking with. In addition, I was very knowledgeable about training animals, and I had a great time working with their pets. The bottom line, however, was that I was totally honest with the clients. If I could teach a dog to do something, then I would work with him until the training was completed. Some of the other trainers would tell the client that they could take the dog and turn him into an obedient guard-trained dog and it was a dachshund. Perhaps they are currently wealthier than I, but I can go to bed at night and sleep soundly.

The training years were very demanding. There were nights when I would go out in snow and ice to evaluate a dog and there would be no money coming in because the owner had to "think it over." Then the next night I would sign up five or six clients. There were certainly a lot of highs and lows.

I remember one of my clients commenting to me, "Ya know, Warren, the reason I hired you was because of the way you dressed."

"The way I was dressed?" I thought. Most likely I was wearing cowboy boots, jeans, and a torn-up old shirt. The client then said that I was the only trainer evaluating the dog who got off the couch and onto his hands and knees and actually touched the dog, played with the dog, and worked with the dog. All the other trainers came to the house in suits and sport jackets. They were just selling something, not offering anything of value.

I would say that 90 percent of the dogs we were training at that point completed the training process in the six- to eight-week time span. However, I did have some dogs that I evaluated at six to eight weeks that needed fourteen, eighteen, and up to six months to complete the training. Regardless, I stuck to my price. I believe that was how we grew. It was word of mouth, with one person saying to another, "You can trust this guy." Soon I was going on evaluations where I would be the only person being considered because I came so highly recommended. And in many cases it turned out that I was retraining pets for clients who had already spent a fortune to have their dog trained by someone else. After the original trainer disappeared and the dog was not acting up to par, the owner would then call me in to get the job done. Sometimes they wanted me to give them a discount based on the fact that they had already spent money to have their dog trained. In reality, the dog was never trained in the first place. I always wondered why people would think I'd give them a discount when I didn't do anything wrong! It was amazing how many retrains we were doing at that point. A lot of companies were really ripping off the clients.

Another interesting aspect of the training was the element of surprise. I would go to evaluate the dog never knowing what I was walking into. Would the dog be as sweet as Benji or would I open the door and find Cujo the devil dog coming at me? And no one would ever admit that their dog was aggressive. When a client called up, Fay would ask if the dog had any aggressive tendencies, and I would enter the house and find the dog had been trained by the Gestapo.

I remember specifically one day I went out to evaluate an Airedale. I am a huge fan of Airedales. A lot of people do not realize what great dogs they are. However, the one I went to see was extremely aggressive. When I walked into the house, the dog was sniffing around, which was normal. The client asked me how I was going to evaluate his pet, and I told him I was going to take him outside for a little walk to see what kind of response I got. I put the dog on a leash and the dog went absolutely ballistic! He lost total control of his bowels and urinated all over me—and all over the owner, who said to me, "Well, that's the problem. When I put him on a leash, he just *freaks out* and tries to kill you. So we never put him on a leash and I wanted to see how he would act with you." The dog was just phobic, and it took months and months to resolve the problem, but eventually the dog adjusted to walking on a leash and became a well-behaved pet.

I could probably tell you hundreds of stories about people who called up with really aggressive dogs, but because you're an animal trainer they assume the animal won't bite you. I guess I should have worn a shirt that said "Animal Trainer" so the dog could read it.

At that time we took clients from all over—Brooklyn, New Jersey, Long Island, Staten Island, Queens, the Bronx, Connecticut. It made no difference where the client was located. I was driving about 150,000 miles a year just based on the traveling we did to see the clients.

Master Dog Training took me to some really incredible areas—and by that I mean places where I was really scared. I would be walking up three or four stories in a tenement to train someone's dog and I was stepping over junkies, and I don't even know if half the people I stepped over were alive. When I became a peace officer, I had to carry a gun twenty-four hours a day. I always wore my gun in an ankle holster. I recall being called out to the South Bronx to train a dog. I was in my Duster when the car broke down. I must say I am not a coward, but neither am I a hero. I'm just confident about myself. This situation, however, was a different story. I actually took out my gun, cocked it, and kept it in my lap. I would not get out of the car until I finally flagged down a patrol car. The officer even pushed me to a different area before we got out of the car to talk. You know you are really in a bad area when the police won't get out of the car!

Another odd place Master Dog Training took me to was a boat dock. This was on Long Island in the Amity Harbor area. Remember the Amityville Horror movies? Well, this was "training horror"! I was waiting to meet the client on this dock when out of the fog came a little rubber raft. I had my attaché case because I was going to be doing an evaluation and I hopped aboard the raft. Now, this was in the middle of winter, so the air was freezing and the water was icy cold. Well, the guy rowed for a good ten, fifteen minutes over to this island where there were only two houses and—you guessed it—the neighbors were fighting over the dog running around the property. We did some perimeter training, which is teaching the dog to stay within a certain area of property. It was a lot of fun, but the entire time I worked on this job I had to allow an extra twenty minutes: ten minutes to row out there, and another ten to row back.

In the early seventies, due to the economy, it was common for young married couples to live on boats—and I'm not talking houseboats; I'm talking thirty-foot cabin cruisers. They would hook up to a dock and pay a small monthly rental fee. Having purchased the boat for about ten thousand dollars, living on it would allow them the opportunity to save lots of money. They would live there a couple of years and then buy a house. On several occasions, I went out to the boats to do the training. Some of these cruisers were very nice, but others I was scared just walking onto for fear the boat would sink. It was an interesting group of people.

I once received a call for guard-dog training at a cemetery in Queens, New York, that was experiencing a lot of vandalism. When the call came in—"Hello, this is XX Cemetery and we need guard dogs"—I kept thinking to myself, "Even after you're dead, you need a dog to protect you?" Apparently, people were breaking into the mausoleums and stealing jewelry and gold and knocking over the stones. To deter the vandalism, I trained about four or five animals to patrol the perimeter as protection dogs with the guards. It was hard for me to understand how *dogs* could frighten people more than the consequences of disturbing the eternal sleep of the dead!

I actually trained a guard dog on the Lower East Side of Manhattan that was in such a bad area that the antiques shop actually had a sign in the window that said "No Cash Accepted! Credit

Cards or Checks Only!" This shop was owned by an elderly Jewish couple. They were so nervous about being there that they felt the need for a guard dog.

I even trained for individual police officers. They worked different shifts and were fearful that their wives were home alone with their families. I gave them a super special price because I knew what they were going through, and we formed this group class. We met every Tuesday and Thursday. At the same time I was working with the animals in Brewster, New York. I would get back to Long Island just in time for the police classes to start and Fay would have a sandwich all ready for me.

Attacking in Russian

I once received a call from a gentleman who wanted his dog trained to be a guard dog. I was always a little skeptical of people who wanted guard dogs; I wanted to be sure that there was a legitimate need. It was like giving someone a loaded weapon. If they didn't know how to use it, or didn't use it properly, it was dangerous. Yet if a guard dog is used correctly, it could fill a dire need for protection. So I interviewed the man over the phone and the need for a guard dog appeared real. He told me he owned a grocery store in Brownsville, Brooklyn, which was not the nicest neighborhood. There were lots of robberies and murders, and the store itself had been broken into several times already. The store was open nearly twenty-four hours a day and he was a little nervous. He did, in fact, carry a gun, and had received a New York Police Gun Permit. I figured if the NYPD approved him for a permit, then I saw no reason why I shouldn't train his dog to protect him and his grocery store.

In order to assess his needs and before anything could be done, it was essential for me to meet with the store owner, the dog, and take a look at the surroundings he wanted the dog to protect. Consequently, a week later, I met with the Brooklyn grocer. He owned a really old-time Brooklyn grocery store with tin ceilings. The store was relatively large for that area and he sold a variety of products, in addition to a vast amount of beer. Noticing some unsavory characters who frequented the store, I told the grocer, "What we're going to have to do with the dog is teach him to be extra good around people, because he will be by your side the majority of the time. You want the dog to be 'kid friendly' because you draw a neighborhood clientele, and it's important that they feel it's OK to come over and pet him. At the same time, we will have to teach the dog a couple of different words to ward off the wrong people. One word would serve to put the dog on guard and the other word would cause the dog to actually bite." At the time, most trainers were training dogs to respond to German commands, but I felt that every burglar in America knew this and thus there was a good chance they knew which commands to use. So, I asked the grocer to come up with two words that would never be used in the store; that way there would never be the chance that the dog would attack an innocent person.

Jokingly, he said, "Let's train the dog in Russian," and sure enough, that was the language we chose. One of the words we used was "malchik," which is Russian for boy. Fay picked that word because she had taken Russian in high school. It took about six months of solid training to get the response I was looking for. I wanted a sharp dog for this task, because Mr. Robertson was a heck of a nice man with a genuine problem. I worked with the dog in the morning and in the evening in order to solidify the basic training and so he would have total control over the dog. Then, I had to hire several agitators. (An agitator is a person who agitates the dog so we could teach the dog to attack or to become angry.) I used different agitators, ranging in race and size to best challenge the dog. As I said, it took a good six months for the dog to respond the way I wanted, but I was very pleased by how far he came. One of the challenging parts of the training was that, in his store, Mr. Robinson had a very high counter, and the dog would have to be able to clear the counter in case of an emergency.

After the training, I wanted to stage a break-in at different times of the day. Mr. Robinson made arrangements with the local police precinct so I wouldn't get shot. I would break in wearing hidden attack-dog clothing, like extra garments under the clothing, to get the most effective response possible. We simulated this several times, and then I didn't hear from Mr. Robinson. Then one day I received a call from him. "Thank you, Warren," he said. "There was a robbery attempt last night. I gave the dog his command and I told the burglar that I had an attack dog on hand. The man responded that he had a gun and he did not care. I then gave the dog his second command and he was on the man faster than he could even think about going for his gun. The dog was on his arm, and I was able to get involved and disarm him without having shots fired. I was safe, the dog was safe, and the man was apprehended by the police."

That's pride. That was teaching the dog what it had to do. This dog loved this man, and this man loved this dog, and perhaps the dog would have protected him without the solid training. Still, I like to take a little credit for it.

This case was just one of many guard dogs I trained over a period of years in New York, Connecticut, and New Jersey. Some of the dogs I worked with were at department stores and gas stations. All were well cared for and did incredible jobs for their owners. The workman's compensation insurance I was required to carry for this type of training was on the high side, but we literally did hundreds of these dogs who all, at one time or another, came through for their owners.

Sebastian the Urinating Husky

I will never forget Sebastian the husky. It was early on in my career, while we were still living in Long Beach. Obviously, dogs were not allowed on the beach, but in the wintertime, when the snow was deep, we would sneak dogs on all the time for training purposes. This, however, was not the wintertime. It was a beautiful warm spring evening with the sun setting on the blue ocean. It was one of those gorgeous days that you just die for in New York. I was going to be working with a dog named Sebastian, a Siberian husky. So I decided, due to the incredible weather, I would take him down to the beach in the Long Beach area.

One of the problems Sebastian was having was that he loved to run, but he had some difficulty with the coming back part. It was such a beautiful evening and I thought, "Thank God, I don't work behind a desk and I work for myself." I could stay out on the beach and work with Sebastian for as long as I liked. Well, we started practicing the basic commands: heel, sit, stay, and come, and he was doing absolutely fine. I was walking him on a lunge line or a light line, which is a very long leash, and again he was doing great. Now was the big test; I was going to be taking him off the lead and working him without the leash to get the response that was necessary.

Well, we were walking down toward this open area of the beach, and there was this young couple enjoying themselves. This scene was right out of *Blue Lagoon*, and this couple was engaged in doing what young couples normally do on a blanket on a beautiful spring evening. So, Sebastian and I were walking along, and all of a sudden Sebastian bolted and ran up to the couple and proceeded to lift his leg and pee all over the man. I could do nothing but turn my head and laugh. I mean, what could I do at that point? Then it occurred to me that this guy might be six feet six and three hundred pounds and, acting really macho in front of his girlfriend, not too thrilled about having urine all over his head. Well, he stood up and yelled across the beach, "Is that dog yours?" To which I replied, "I never saw that dog before in my life." After rounding up Sebastian, we trekked farther down the beach, where I put him back on leash and he responded well. The couple was now out of sight, and I felt confident that Sebastian would not repeat his escapade, so I took him off the leash once again. Sure enough, out of the blue, Sebastian bolted again, racing back to the couple and deftly urinating on the man's head once again. The man took off in pursuit of Sebastian, and I took off in pursuit of the man. It was quite the Keystone Kop chase. Eventually Sebastian became a well-behaved dog. And as far as I know he has not peed on anyone since.

Happily Ever After

One day I received a call from a man named Bill who said he headed a charity called Assistance Dogs International. He had heard about the work I was doing with people with disabilities and their pets and wanted to meet. We met and he explained that there was a tremendous need to train people how to do what I was doing (back then it was called Dogs for the Handicapped; now it's called Pet Facilitated Therapy). I assumed it was already being done and my work was not so unusual, but found out I was actually quite progressive.

I was told about a unique place in Brewster, New York, that was a school for "crisis children"—kids who had major problems in their life. It was a farm atmosphere, and the classes I was to teach had nothing to do with the school but focused more on the location. Assistance Dogs International had several Ph.D. students in the group who wanted to learn how to do this type of training so they could go back to their respective states and organizations and offer these services. A.D.I. provided a service that was very needed, but my gut reaction, my animal instinct, said be wary of Bill. I was not a big fan of his. Regardless, I would drive up to Brewster twice a week to work with these people and the dogs and cats that were rescued from shelters to be trained and given to people in need.

Training a dog for a handicapped owner.

This work gave me the opportunity to meet some incredible individuals. A woman who suffered from epilepsy called from Worcester, Massachusetts, after hearing that dogs could detect seizures. She wanted to know if I could train a dog to respond to epilepsy. For her, the problem was that in the past, during a seizure, she would either fall or pass out and people on the street would assume that she was either a junkie or an alcoholic.

Hers would become the first dog of its kind trained in the country. Working with one of the dogs we rescued, I observed that when a seizure would start to overcome her, the dog would start to react first. I guess they pick up an odor. That wasn't training; that was just a natural instinct on the dog's part. My job was to train the dog to guide her over to a soft area where she was able to sit or lie down. The dog also wore a special orange collar or harness with the name of the owner's doctor and the type of medical problem she had—in this case, epilepsy. She stayed in touch with me, and over the years, the dog did an incredible job for her.

It was also at this time that I was training some of the first (I call them) "pickup" dogs, for people who were either quadriplegic or paraplegic and unable to pick something up if they dropped it from their wheelchair, or retrieve something like a telephone. The dogs were taught to respond for these individuals, some of whom lived in senior citizens' housing. The apartments of these disabled people had a string on the floor, so if someone passed out they could pull the string and set off an alarm. Therefore, teaching the dogs to pull these strings was a very important part of whatever training we were doing. Again, if someone dropped his keys or a bottle or whatever, the dog would pick the item up and give it back to the owner. Some people didn't think this was a big deal. "All right, so the dog walks next to a wheelchair; what's the big deal?" they'd say. What these people failed to understand was that doorways at that time were not as wide as they are today and people couldn't get out as much as they do now. It was a real challenge to teach these dogs how to respond to elevators and how quickly the doors opened and closed, and how to pull someone away if the elevator doors were closing on them. They had to learn how to maneuver their bodies in front of the wheelchair to get into narrow spaces. It was some fascinating work at this point, and the one thing that helped me more than anything else was that whenever I trained a dog, for whatever purpose, I would try to emulate that person. If a dog had to respond to a wheelchair, then when I was training, the wheelchair is where I would be. If I had to teach a dog to respond to a hearing impaired individual, I would put cotton in my ears so that my hearing was impaired. The only way to get the response I ultimately wanted was to put myself in the position where the dog had to respond.

One guy I met was an elderly man who had lost both legs. When we first met, he was as crude as they come. If he wasn't cussing, he was downing another beer. Frank used to enjoy his fishing trips, but somehow over the years things changed. Life didn't hold the same zest for him as it once had, and now he lived in a building that was run by Catholic charities in Queens, New York. He was not a well-groomed man. His hair was unkempt, his fingernails were filthy, and, quite honestly, his apartment stunk. He never left the apartment, neglected his own food shopping, and had no friends. We all felt that it would be good for him to have a dog; now, all I had to do was to convince *him*.

After getting to know Frank, I found out he was an old dog lover from way back when. After many meetings, he agreed, but he had a specific dog in mind. He wasn't the poodle type; he liked the heartier, more robust breeds, the ones others found unappealing.

That was going to be my first task—find the dog. Then I had to train it. The training involved teaching the dog to work with a wheelchair in and out of doors and elevators. Also, the dog had to be taught to pick up any dropped items. Because of Frank's hearing loss, the animal would also have to be trained to respond to doorbells, alarms, and even a boiling tea kettle.

Well, for Frank I found a long (very long) basset hound named Fred. Fred was unwanted and had ended up in the animal shelter, set to be destroyed, because not everyone thinks full-grown bassets are cute and cuddly. I knew it was the perfect match; you see, the dog was just as tough as the guy he was going to live with.

Frank and Fred hit it off immediately. Through the training, Fred came to understand that Frank did not hear very well, and in no time at all, Fred was letting Frank know when the tea kettle was whistling and when someone was at the door. Even *I* was surprised at how well the two responded to each other. Then something strange happened that was totally unexpected.

When I went back three weeks later to follow up, I walked into the apartment and almost fainted. There, sitting in the wheelchair, was Frank with his hair combed, his nails cleaned, and wearing an outfit out of *GQ*. Astonished, I asked what had caused such a drastic change. He explained that he would run out of dog food and would need to go to the store. He would meet people on the street who would comment on Fred, some of whom were attractive senior women. Consequently, he started grooming himself and spending more time outside. He started having dinner with many of these people and ultimately remarried and last I heard lived happily with his new wife and, of course, Fred.

The man who ran Assistance Dogs International turned out to be a shyster whose goals weren't as altruistic as they appeared. I didn't get my salary for about eight months and he beat me out of a lot of money at the end. On the "plus" side, I was able to create some new approaches to training that no one had ever done before, and they restored dignity to many peoples' lives. I think the bottom line was letting the dogs teach *me*, watching the way *they* reacted, then using that to establish what approach I might need in the training for the individual problem.

Mother's Little Helper

A young lady named Wendy called our office, a new bride. During our conversation, it was a little bit hard to understand her at first because Wendy was hearing impaired; however, she was not deaf. She and her husband had gotten a dog and they wanted it trained for basic obedience, which I did. A little bit down the road, her hearing impairment worsened, and her doctors diagnosed that she was going to be totally deaf within the next couple of years. Around this time Wendy became pregnant, and her big fear became how was she going to care for her child if she couldn't hear the baby crying when it was hungry or when it was sick or not feeling well, as well as other things that hearing people take for granted?

For example, how would she know if someone was at the door?

How would she hear the water for tea boiling, or fire alarms ringing? All of these sensory details that we take for granted were very important to Wendy in order for her to be a good mom. Hearing Ear dogs were not a major option at this point—there were possibly one or two such organizations in existence nationally, and they weren't providing assistance on a wide enough scale to be accessible to the average person.

I undertook this challenge. There was very little of this type of training being done. There were no textbooks on the subject to consult, and the "experts" were me and someone in Sioux City! One of the fascinating aspects of my career was the fact that I worked with people and pets in their *home environment*. And often in many of the homes I went into, one or more family members were physically challenged. So it never occurred to me that getting a deaf child and a dog to respond to each other was in any way unusual. I'd been doing it my entire career; I thought everyone was doing it. Today, we know them as assistance dogs or service dogs, but when I first started they didn't have a name.

The birth of a child should be a happy time, so more than anything, I wanted Wendy to experience the same joy as any expectant mother. So, in the months ahead I invested a lot of time with Wendy, building *her* sense of security while getting her *dog* to respond to the necessary commands. I'd get the dog to go between Wendy and the sound; for example, if the doorbell rang, the dog would go to the door and bark. Obviously, Wendy wouldn't hear that, but the dog would then run to Wendy and go back to the door, back and forth, until Wendy knew the doorbell had rung and responded to it. The same basic principle was used to teach the dog to respond when the baby was crying, and we used a doll and the sound effects tape of a baby crying to get the response we wanted while Wendy was still pregnant. We added tea kettles, telephones (in conjunction with a TTY machine), and alarms, and were able to get her dog to respond to everyday sounds. It wasn't the fine-tuning of some of the Hearing Ear dogs that are being used today, but the dog served incredibly well for Wendy and gave her tremendous confidence in her role as a new mother.

A few years later, Wendy and her family moved to New Jersey, where she organized a seminar for other mothers who had disabilities and showed them how to compensate. She even asked me to conduct a seminar. It was certainly gratifying to be involved with this type of training before it even had a name or was done by a lot of people.

The Marc Wolinski Story

The year was 1981 and I was still working with Assistance Dogs International. I trained the trainers from all over the world at a farm in Brewster, New York, called Green Chimneys, which also served as a home for troubled youths.

This was my first introduction to a man named Marc Wolinski. One of the chairmen of this organization actually called me himself and told me about a father living in Oceanside looking to purchase a dog for his son. This would need to be a special dog because the man's son had Down's syndrome, a genetic defect that caused mental retardation. The parents had contacted Assistance Dogs International, and the organization had in turn contacted me.

The boy lived in my hometown and after meeting Marc, well, we shared a special bond. Marc was eighteen years old and incredibly bright. He had an older brother whom he adored and emulated. I said I would do the training at no cost to the family, because it felt like the right thing to do. We started the process by searching for the perfect dog. At that time the Broadway show *Annie* was very popular and he only wanted a dog that resembled "Sandy." So we scoured the shelters and the pounds and came up with a mixed terrier whom Marc named Buffy. There was extensive training involved because ultimately the goal was not getting the dog to respond to me but to respond to Marc. Marc lived in a suburban area with lots of kids, and kids could be pretty cruel; Marc did not have many close friendships. My thoughts on this subject were that if I could get the dog to do certain tricks, it would in turn be a catalyst in helping Marc make friends.

We started out with some basic training where I taught the dog to heel, sit, stay, and come—and later to fetch a ball and to sit and beg. I then taught Marc how to get Buffy to respond the same way. At the same time, I also instilled in Marc the responsibility of caring for his pet by grooming, brushing, and other pet ownership tasks. We worked for several weeks on this. Buffy was very bright, and Marc was an astute learner. Clearly, Marc was not lacking intelligence, it was just a matter of a meeting of the minds and that the dog understand how to respond to Marc's commands. And watching them together, it was as if the dog knew that there was something special about Marc.

The tricks we taught Buffy ultimately made Marc a hit in the neighborhood. This kid, who would go outside to play and then be shunned by the other kids, was now a crowd pleaser, thanks to Buffy. In walking the dog, the twosome would stop and meet people, casually interacting with neighbors and friends—unimaginable without Buffy.

It was a lot of work at the time, and there had not been a lot of research on the subject. I remember a quote in a local newspaper from a pediatrician at the National Institute of Child Health and Human Development in Maryland, skeptical of the therapy's value. He said, "I do question the emotional support a dog can provide. How do you measure a dog's emotional capability and how can it be transmitted? The whole thing is based on a tenuous assumption."

I liked the word *assumption*, because you know what happens when you assume. The bottom line was it worked. And perhaps if more of these professionals spent time out of the laboratory, going "hands on" in the real world and watching the results, they would understand.

Marc's father was a professor at a major university on Long Island and his mother was also well educated. The Wolinskis disagreed entirely with the skeptics, and approved heartily of the therapy and its effects upon Marc. They saw their son embracing responsibility and being rewarded with companionship. They were making their statements based on their experiences and they said, "It works!" And it does work. Having had the opportunity since that time of working with several different children living with Down's syndrome and various other types of mental disorders, I have found that dogs are successful catalysts for establishing relationships and in providing emotional support. As I said, this was in 1981; to this day I still get cards from Marc, who is working independently on Long Island and is doing very well. I'd like to think that I had something to do with his ability to pursue a normal lifestyle. It was truly a fascinating relationship. There existed a great bond between Marc and Buffy, and it will go on to live in my memory for many years to come.

Mafia Dogs

On the occasions when I sit down and watch "Biography" on A&E—every time they profile the New York and New Jersey mobsters—it's déjà vu for me. In fleeting glimpses, I'll say, "Oh, see that guy? He was a client of mine." Or, "Look at that dog in the background; I trained that dog."

A lot of people have a fascination with the Mafia lifestyle, and that's why movies like *The Godfather*, and more recently *Donnie Brasco* and *Casino*, do so well. It was an intriguing time for me when I was drawn into their world. They all used the same accountant, the same attorney, and, likewise I suppose, one of my titles became animal trainer to the mob.

It all began in the early seventies when I received a call from a guy named Walter. When I asked his last name before setting up the appointment, he gruffly shot back at me, "All you need to know is Walter." I arrived outside a waterfront mansion in Nassau Shores on Long Island, a well-known area for wise guys! With barely a nod, a thickset guy who was standing watch escorted me to the door where Walter met me. Walter and a rather intimidating man I'll call Mr. Big sat down and watched me while I evaluated his Great Dane. I quoted a price and presented a contract, which their demeanor suggested was unnecessary. "Do the job and you'll get paid," they said. I went on to make sure that this dog was a Lassie clone, and then went above and beyond! By the end of the eight weeks of training, Walter and I became friendly and I shared with him that, being a newlywed, I was using the training fee to buy a dining room set for my wife. Later he handed me an envelope stuffed with extra cash, with a note, "For the dog—and enjoy your new dining room." Until Mr. Big died years later, I didn't really know who he was. But there he was on the front page of *Newsday*, his passing reported in detail along with a picture of his estate and his Great Dane.

Over the next few years, I trained more dogs for the wise guys. And they were probably some of the best clients I ever had. Remember, I was there to work with the animals; I wasn't involved in their other businesses. They got what they paid for, I made sure of that. I didn't see people—I saw a leash and a dog and just kept my mouth shut. Thanks to a very close friend of mine who told me how to handle the scenario, it worked well.

As I think over my Mafia stories, I'm always hesitant about mentioning who and what, where and why. But there were some fascinating times—from strictly a business point of view. Once, I was called into a home in Brooklyn, which, from the outside, looked like a typical brownstone in a slightly rundown section of Bay Ridge. (By the way, if you're looking for the best pizza in America, this mostly Italian neighborhood is where you'll find it!) As I was going into the basement of this building I couldn't help noticing a couple of, I want to call them gorillas, hanging around outside. They weren't really menacing. More like curious doughboys in their really nice Hawaiian shirts and slacks.

When I approached, they said, "Yo, where youse going?"

"My name's Warren," I told them, "and I'm here to see so and so." I met the guy who owned the dog, and with a look around, it was unmistakable that I was training a guard dog for a bookie joint. The tip-off? When he led me downstairs, I saw twenty to thirty telephones and desks all over the basement, and a heavy cloud of smoke hung in the air. I can assure you: Cigar smoke and bottles of Anisette were a sight and smell that will stay in my head forever. The telephones were constantly ringing and an assortment of guys were always hunched over, taking bets nonstop. This was a twenty-four-hour operation.

Interestingly enough, they had an Italian dog—a breed that was unknown at this point, called the Neapolitan mastiff. It's very powerful and probably the only dog that knocked me on my ass when I was doing guard dog work with him. He was that strong. He was a great dog, and he looked as if he should be wearing a fedora and smoking a cigar himself! I went to this place several times to work with his dog and even brought my trainers there as agitators to reinforce the training.

As I was leaving one time, the guy I was seeing asked me, "Do you bet on the ponies?"

"Not really," I replied.

"Too bad," he said, " 'cuz I have this great tip for ya." He passed it on as I half listened, not thinking anything of it. At that time my mother would place a bet once in a while. Since she was working and making a good amount of money, it was just a goof to her. That popped into my mind while I was driving back on the Belt Parkway. "What was that horse's *name*? I'll call my mother and I'll give her the tip; it came straight from this big bookie in Bay Ridge, it's worth a shot." I pulled off the road to a little newsstand. I picked up a newspaper and looked at the racing form in the back. It's the sixth race, I remembered, while scanning the horses that were running and trying to find a familiar name. Here's the one! So I called my mother, she was all excited, everyone was excited because they got this great tip. My mother bet a couple hundred dollars on the horse, she called her boss, who invested a bundle, and the next day everyone lost their money.

When I went back to see the Bay Ridge bookie, the guy said, "How did you make out? Did you ever bet on the horse?"

"Well," I said, "I didn't bet on this horse, but I gave the tip to my mother and they all bet and lost."

"Lost?" he said. "That horse came in and paid incredibly well." It turned out that I gave them the wrong horse, so that didn't work out too well. Anyway, it took me about twelve weeks to train the dog, and at the end I got a really nice cash tip. And as a result, the business just started pouring in. I'd get more and more calls. In the neighborhood it seemed strange to see these men, not working regular jobs, hanging around all day with pockets full of cash.

They usually sounded uncomfortable on the phone. For instance, one day at the kennel I fielded a call from a guy I swear sounded exactly like Sonny Corleone. "Mmm, I gotta dog, y'know an' you need to train him, 'cuz he's a puppy—whaddya call, a Doberman." In reply, I explained to him that the kind of training I preferred doing was in the home, where I could work with him and the dog at the same time. "Naw, I'm a busy man, got things to take care of out onna road for a few months. Can't we take care of it witcha? I'll make it worth your time, unnerstan?" I told him to come on down so I could evaluate the dog and see what we could do. If we proceeded with the training, when he came back I could give him a basic refresher course with the dog at the same time. A few days later a short, skinny guy with dark glasses and a mustache shows up with an adorable Doberman puppy that I fell in love with immediately. I was up-front with the owner. "Understand, this is a very expensive proposition, having me do the training at the kennel in addition to the follow-up course when you come back. Obviously there are boarding fees for the two to three months you're gone; so you're looking at about a $1,500 deposit as an advance."

"No problem," he replied, lifting his shirt, under which were stacks—and I mean *stacks*—of hundred-dollar bills stuck into his belt. I couldn't count all the stacks, but I know I had never seen so much money in my life. Somewhere in the conversation I said to him, "By the way, what do you do for a living?"

His exact words to me were: "Hear this once: You never ask a man what he does for a living." Anyway, he paid me the cash up-front and took off. We began working with the dog, and for a couple of months I would get a weekly call from the owner telling me he was in North Carolina, or here or there. The dog was incredibly well trained, so much so that it got to the point where he was bored of the basic training, and on my own I started doing some advance work with him. Meanwhile, the frequency of the owner's calls started to diminish, now coming once a month. After three or four months, the boarding bill alone was way over what this guy paid me as an advance.

I intercepted his next call saying, "Look, can we clear up the balance for your dog? The initial deposit was an estimate based on you being gone for a couple of months. It's been twice that long. Can you send me a check or, if you like, we're set up so you can give me a credit card number over the phone."

He answered, "No, my brother will stop by and take care of it."

Around ten or eleven o'clock the next morning, I swear to you, a car pulls up to the kennel and out of the car walks a guy who looks *exactly* like the guy I originally met. I mean an identical twin, who hands me more money, again in cash. To this day I don't know if this was the same guy or what. Anyway, it was about this time that a major crime figure in the New York area was killed—a regular mob hit, two bullets behind the head, somewhere in Staten Island. The timing coincided with this latest trip to the kennel to pay me. As it came to be, after six or seven months of this going back and forth, I never heard from him again. There is no doubt in my mind that this guy was a hit man for the mob; I'm totally convinced. And months went by without ever hearing from him, or interestingly enough, from his "brother." To this day, I still believe they were probably one and the same. And he left behind the only one who knew—this great dog that, fortunately, everyone loved, who was adopted by one of my trainers.

On another occasion, at a home in Nassau Shores, while evaluating a dog owned by a guy I'll call Jim and discussing my fee, the guy pointed to a coffee table and said, "You see this bowl?" And there sat this bowl, on display like a centerpiece, filled with white powder—literally thousands of dollars' worth of cocaine piled high—and he gestured, saying, "Here, take this as payment and whatever you want, just come to me."

And I answered, "No, that's OK." Ultimately he did pay me in cash, there was no problem; but every time I went there he would try to pay me in drugs, as did many of my clients at that time in the seventies. But it was simply not a temptation for me.

Besides the social clubs where the Mafia purportedly gathered, an acquaintance of mine owned a bar in Queens that, for a time, was a popular watering hole for capos, or Mafia soldiers. The bar had run its course, and on this particular night, there was a party to close it. When Fay and I arrived there was an eerie feeling in the air. I mean, people were usually two to three deep at the bar, but this evening it wasn't crowded. Glancing around, there were maybe five or six couples as we joined my best friend and his wife there. Two of the women who were seated with these guys said, "Hey, Warren, how're you doing?" At first I thought they recognized me from TV because, at this point, I had made some on-camera appearances. But then I realized I had trained their dogs. They introduced me to their husbands, whom I had not met previously.

The uneasiness heightened when no one else came into the bar that night. Fay had a funny feeling she couldn't shake and I teased her, "If you hear any shots, duck!"—jokingly, not meaning anything by it. We timed our stay just long enough that our host wouldn't be offended and then left. Within a week of that night two out of the four guys were found dead at different locations. They were Mob-style hits, one in the Bronx and I think one in Staten Island. This time, it was a little too close to home. I was grateful for their patronage and for the most part they were good to deal with on my level. I never got into their business, nor they into mine. I did my job and, I guess, they did theirs.

The Man Who Taught His Dog to Win Big Money

It was the mid-seventies and it was one of the first jobs that called me out to exclusive Park Avenue. The customer actually had another home on the eastern end of Long Island in addition to his magnificent Park Avenue penthouse. To say the least, I was in awe. I can't recall the man's last name, but his first name was Stewart and he owned an incredible German shepherd. When I walked into the house, I was truly impressed. Not only was the apartment gorgeous, but so was his very elegant wife. She was from Yugoslavia, and the night I arrived, she made her entrance in a ravishing ball gown and was wrapped in an incredibly stunning (but disgusting to me) floor-length lynx coat. Breezing by on her way out for an evening on the town, she blew her husband a kiss from Cartier-bejeweled fingers. After she left, Stewart and I sat down and talked about their adorable German shepherd puppy, who had some basic problems. The puppy was doing some chewing, jumping up on people, being annoying, pulling the owner down the block, disagreeing with other dogs it met on the street, and stealing Chinese food right out of the owner's hands.

It took about six weeks to complete the basic obedience training, and at the time I charged about $500. Then the man asked me, "How much would you charge to teach him a trick?"

"Well, it depends on what kind of trick and how long it would take," I answered.

Stewart then explained in detail what he wanted his dog to do. "I want to put down three objects on the floor that look exactly alike. Then I want the dog to stop, and pick up one of the objects when I do something on cue that would not be recognizable to other people."

So I paused, then said, "You mean, like those dogs on TV that walk in a circle and pick out a number . . . is that what you're asking me?"

"Yeah, something like that. How do you get the dog to respond?"

I told him that there were several ways to do it. "Some people use really discreet hand signals, while others might use facial gestures to prompt the dog." In the past, when I was training dogs in this way, I would use a click or a swallow in my voice to cue the dog to stop. It was intense training, but it could be done.

Stewart then pressed me for an answer. "What's the charge to do that?"

"What's the purpose of this training?"

"Well," Stewart hesitated. "Can I talk to you man to man?"

"Absolutely," I said.

"I'm a gambling man," he responded. This was no shock to me. He resembled Bugsy Siegel, complete with a big stogie and a three-piece suit. Again, he repeated, "How much would this service cost?"

I told him this would entail extensive training a couple of times per week and then he would have to practice with the dog, diligently. He replied that he would be willing to do anything, that he was ready to put the time in for a gambling dog. I recall saying to him that I needed to think about the price and I walked out. I went home and discussed it with Fay. I knew this would be time consuming, and I thought I would quote him a price that would surely be rejected, because I wasn't really sure I wanted to do this for the guy. There was something about it that just wasn't quite kosher. I called him the next day and quoted him $1,500. I assumed he would say, "Are you crazy, Warren? You only charged me five hundred dollars for basic obedience training." Instead he said, "Fine, that was very reasonable." I always had a problem of underquoting, but I hoped this would cover all the time necessary to turn this animal into a gambling dog.

In any case, I went on to teach the dog to pick out the object when the man swallowed, and we got to the point that the dog was consistently picking right on target. I told Stewart that since he was a gambler, he should let the dog make some mistakes and pick up the wrong object; that way people around him would assume that nobody was perfect. Well, Stewart took it a few steps further.

A month or two after the training was completed, I met Stewart on the street. He said to me, "You know, Warren, you made me a lot of money!"

"I made you a lot of money?"

Here I was thinking I *charged* him a lot of money and he was telling me how much money I *made* him. He then explained that twice a week he hosted poker games over at the penthouse with different guys from Wall Street, and they were all gambling men. He had put a spin on what I had taught him—that is, teaching the dog to pick up what I would tell him to pick up when the man swallowed. He would put down a ten-dollar bill, a twenty-dollar bill, and a fifty-dollar bill. Then he would tell the guys, "My dog will always pick up the fifty-dollar bill." Well, all the men thought that was the craziest thing; how would the dog know the difference between a fifty, a twenty, and a ten? Understand, that when the man swallowed, the dog would pick up that specific bill no matter what bill it was. His friends would then bet a thousand dollars that the dog would not pick up a fifty twice in a row; Stewart would then let the dog make mistakes. When the pots got really big, he would swallow and the dog would obey, and he would win thousands. I said to myself, "Where did he get this idea? What an imagination!" Years later, I still laugh about that, saying, "Gee, if I only had the guts to do it, because if I could teach *his* dog to do it, *my* dog would be the *ultimate* professional gambler. God knows, I would have retired a long time ago."

I still bump into this mischievous man who taught his dog to win big money!

Love, American Style

I've had some strange calls in my life, but one call bordered on kinky. It wasn't just any crackpot on the phone, it was a former client from Kew Gardens in Queens whose dog I had trained. He started, "Warren, my new wife and I have two dogs now, and we're all having trouble in the bedroom." My first response was, "Call Dr. Ruth and leave me alone!" But I agreed to delve further into the problem, and when I got there, a beautiful German shepherd greeted me along with a normal-looking couple in their fifties. Warily, I asked them what their problem was, and it seemed normal enough: *His* dog did not get along with *her* dog.

It went downhill from there. And the "trigger point" was anytime the couple was trying to have some kind of sexual relationship. Her dog would be very possessive of her and his dog very possessive of him. Apparently, this couple's sexual relations were very important, and whenever they would try to get together the dogs would go bananas if they were in the same room. When I recommended obvious things, like closing the door, they didn't want to do it; they wanted their dogs to be happy, to be around and be part of their lives. So what solution was left, given that I'm the kind of trainer who had to put myself into *every* situation in order to observe and thereby correct the problem? If they thought I was going to *watch*, well then, they were barking up the wrong tree! It was the one behavioral situation I couldn't observe firsthand (and didn't want to!).

Next thing I heard was that they actually went out and bought two adjoining houses in Levittown, Long Island, and every other night they would *alternate* homes, with each dog spending equal amounts of time in the bedroom with them. As long as only one of the dogs was with them in the bedroom at a time, it was OK.

Hey, I just cash the check, folks. But it's always amazing what people will do for their pets.

CELEBRITIES

Rodney Dangerfield

When I received the call he used a different name, which I believe was Jack Roy. He called me himself, which really impressed me. We started chatting and he inquired about my background. Within that conversation, some names were dropped and he asked me if I was famous.

"I guess I'm famous in the animal behavior world," I said, "but that's the only place my fame would be."

He then said, "Well, perhaps you've heard of me."

"Perhaps I have," I said.

"My name is Rodney Dangerfield."

"Oh sure, I'm a big fan of yours. I've enjoyed you for years on 'The Tonight Show.'"

We developed a good rapport, and I remember that when I went over to his apartment, he answered the door in a bathrobe I wouldn't wear if I was a hermit living by myself in the hills of Montana. He was a real down-to-earth guy and I liked that. The time I was there he had an electric jogging machine and his poodle, Kino, had peed on it, causing it to short out. Rodney was waiting for the serviceman to come and fix it. We sat at the table for a good ten minutes and before we even started talking about the dog, he was showing me all his gadgets, including a TV that could make telephone calls. He also ran through a nice repertoire of jokes. I think the best animal joke I ever heard came straight out of Rodney's mouth: "Talk about no respect, my dog closes his eyes before he humps my leg." That is a classic.

I went on to work with his dog and learned that celebrities are difficult to work with sometimes because of their hectic schedules. They're always traveling here and there, so nothing is consistent in the dog's life. Rodney said Kino was leaving "Tootsie Rolls" on the floor and urinating everywhere in his New York apartment. So he actually hired a girl in the building to help with the training. I met with her a few times, and then with Rodney a few times.

I always found it amusing that this tiny little dog would be peeing all over Rodney Dangerfield's house. I just couldn't get the "no respect" line out of my head. Actually, the pooch was lonely *because* Rodney was on the road so much. Kino realized that his problems would get him attention, and if he behaved himself, he'd be ignored. With the young girl taking him to the park and playing with him (as well as Rodney, when he was in town) it worked.

A month or two after the training his secretary gave me a call. "Rodney would like you to come see him at Carnegie Hall or Radio City Music Hall," she said. Fay and I went, and not only did we see the show, but Rodney invited us to join him backstage! After the show we sat in the dressing room with him and had some 7-Up and cheese. It was quite an interesting night. There were all sorts of luminaries: politicians, news anchors, Fortune 500 types, and *me*—the guy who stopped his dog from peeing.

It's just amazing how celebrities relate to their pets.

Al Pacino

Al Pacino. What a guy!

One day I received an odd call. The man said he wanted me to train for someone who was very famous but couldn't reveal his identity. He just wanted me to meet him in the city and from there he would drive me to another location. I would then meet this infamous character and train his dog. By this point in time I had trained a number of dogs for alleged organized crime figures, so I'd learned that it was in my best interest to find out who I was going to see *before* I went and saw him. Otherwise, I could wind up like Jimmy Hoffa.

So I called this guy back and told him I didn't mind going, and I didn't mind working with him, but I had to know who I was going to see. Well, the guy met me in the city and it turned out he was part of Al Pacino's management team. We drove up to Westchester County where Al had this beautiful house overlooking the Hudson River. I remember pulling up the driveway along which was posted a sign that said "Careful Driving! Puppies at Play." Right off the bat I knew I was going to be dealing with a really super guy.

Inside the house I met Al and his two dogs, Lucky and Susie. Fay accompanied me on this trip because she wanted to meet Al. (Do I need to explain why?) It said a lot to us that he chose mixed-breed dogs instead of designer dogs. We chatted and laughed and the one thing I remember about the conversation was that Al kept saying "Did yas eat? Did yas eat?"

It was like being at home with my Jewish mother—I guess Jewish mothers and Italian mothers travel in the same orbit.

Although Al was somewhat shy with humans, Lucky and Susie helped him relax at home. We discussed his puppies and I gave him some advice in terms of what I would recommend for his dogs. We did a little leash work as well. At the time, Al was immersed in his role for the movie *Scarface*, and he was truly living as "Tony Montana." I would look at him and, from one moment to the next, it was like he was two different people. It was truly an astounding transformation.

Anyway, we set up an appointment for the following week at his apartment on Manhattan's Upper East Side. I walked into the apartment and sitting there with Al were Elliot Gould and David Mamet, all playing Atari baseball. I chuckled to myself at the sight of these megastars playing video games.

I started the training process with the two puppies. The dogs were doing well and the training was progressing. But I had a little problem with Al's efforts. I don't think he was really into practicing with his dogs. Sometimes people think you can just hire someone and they'll fix your dog. Well, you can hire someone to fix the electricity, the water pipes, or the woodwork, but no one can fix your dog for you. A pet is a living, emotional thing, and it requires a personal commitment by the owner. In any case, I continued with the lessons, and I believe Al was happy. I moved on and have enjoyed Al's acting even more ever since.

David Letterman Stories

Do dogs take on the personality of their owners? You bet they do! Let me tell you about David Letterman and his infamous dog Bob.

Bob was a chubby shepherd mix, a pretty generic-looking dog who had an incredible personality. He was funny; in fact, he was so funny that I often joked with Dave that if the dog had a space between his teeth, he'd be hosting "Late Night" and Dave would be home chewing pigs' ears.

One morning I received a phone call from a lady named Merrill Markoe. The name meant nothing to me, but she said she was the girlfriend of a famous comedian. They had just moved to an apartment on the Upper East Side of Manhattan from their spacious home in Malibu. In the process of the move, their two dogs, Bob and Stanley, were having difficulty making the adjustment from the laid-back pace of Malibu Beach. The noises and the smells on the streets of New York City were new and threatening to them, so they reacted with excessive barking and growling. And they had problems dealing with other dogs on the street and were becoming aggressive. Overall, their behavior just wasn't what it should be. Merrill told me the name of this famous comedian: David Letterman. I had not heard of David at that point, but friends had told me of his several guest appearances on "The Tonight Show." As with any new client, I quoted Merrill my fee and went to see the dogs. This began a training session that lasted many, many months. Sometimes we worked together at Dave's home in Manhattan; other times, Bob and Stan would be schooled out on eastern Long Island, where Dave and Merrill rented a house. Many of the lessons actually took place right at the NBC studios at 30 Rockefeller Center. Remember, this was before "Late Night with David Letterman." This was "The David Letterman Show," an early morning national talk show on NBC.

I resolved several of the problems Dave and Merrill were having with "The Guys," as they used to call them. I desensitized and socialized them by taking them out for short walks, and hanging out with them on the streets of the Upper East Side. There I was, ten o'clock at night, Lexington and 86th. Prostitutes, homeless people, drug dealers, me, and Dave Letterman's two dogs! By using recorded sound effects, the dogs adjusted to the idea that the noises on the street were not threatening, and they became die-hard New Yorkers. It helped that Bob and Stan worked pretty well together. Dave and Merrill traveled a lot, so my staff and I took care of Bob and Stan while they were away. While in my care at my kennel, Pet Resorts International, their daily routine included school, swimming, and one hour of pet aerobics daily.

Sometimes I had to sneak Bob and Stan into the NBC Studios at "30 Rock"—there was a "no dogs allowed" policy. I even tried wearing dark glasses, hoping people would just assume they were guide dogs. But once in a while I would get busted while reading the *New York Post!*

Clearly, Bob was more Dave's dog and Stanley was closer to Merrill. You could really see that by the tactics Bob employed to get attention. Dave told me one particular story of how Bob stole a frozen fifteen-pound turkey off the countertop. He not only ate the entire thing, probably with some help from Stan, but he left the wrapper on the floor, as if to say, "Hey, Dave, anything for a laugh!" (Merrill was not smiling.) Because of the incredible schedules Dave and Merrill kept, the dogs suffered from separation anxiety. The turkey antic was Bob's way of getting attention, even though it was negative. The bottom line was that Bob and Stan really got along well with each other. They were two great dogs.

Over time, I became a frequent guest on "The David Letterman Show." In fact, there is some dispute as to how "Stupid Pet Tricks" originated. Let me give you *my* version, the only *true* one, and I'm *stickin'* to it!

I was working one day up on the sixth floor at NBC Studios with Dave, Merrill, and two writer/comedians, Will Shriner and Rich Hall. At this point, Bob and Stan had received their diplomas. They heeled and stayed, came when they were called, and basically responded to all the commands that every good dog should. Then Dave challenged me, "Why don't you teach them something different?" So within a few minutes I taught them both to crawl on their bellies, like you would teach a war dog, and Dave cracked up, saying, "Hey, Warren, that's the stupidest thing I've ever seen," and Merrill added, "Boy, that is really dumb." I shot back with, "If you think *that*'s stupid, you should see the tricks some of my other clients have asked me to teach their pets." Whether it was dancing with their dachshund, playing poker with their Pomeranian, or singing with their Siamese, there were really some incredible feats that people wanted their pets to learn. It was

Dave Letterman with girlfriend, and Bob and Stan.

Merrill at that time who said, "Stupid pet tricks. People teach their pets stupid things." And that's how it *really* started.

I went on to make several appearances on the show, one of my most memorable being the night I brought my pig Spotty, and here's how the saga began. I received a call from Barry Sands, then producer for David's show. This was when "Late Night with David Letterman" started. In any case, I got the call on a Tuesday: "Warren, we want to do a segment; how about doing one with a pig on Thursday?" My response was: "I live on Long Island, the show's in New York City, today is Tuesday. Where do you expect me to find a pig by Thursday. By the way, I understand that Seven-Eleven is all sold out." I made some phone calls anyway and found a pig farmer (under "P" in my Rolodex) in upstate New York. I called him up and made a deal. I told him NBC was willing to pay $35 for the pig, I would pick up the little piglet and bring him down (driving three hours each way), do the Letterman show with him, and then I would bring him back; he could keep the $35. Well, once again my great business skills surfaced—obviously the farmer was as happy as a pig in . . . you know.

I picked up the ten-week-old piglet on Wednesday morning and spent all day with him. I then said to my wife, "You know, in order for this pig to really bond with me, and for him to respond at all, I'd better stay a little later at the kennel." So I spent the night and slept with the pig, and once you sleep with a pig, he becomes yours. The next day he responded well to the tricks I taught him. But getting to the studio was mayhem. Driving the Long Island Expressway in a 1970 Duster with a pig in the passenger seat had even blasé New Yorkers doing a double take! On the air, Dave joked about sleeping with pigs and got quite a laugh at my expense. We actually christened the pig during the show. It was black and white; so, being as creative as we were, Dave and I came up with the name Spotty. Spotty and I performed our few pig tricks. We sat, we stayed, and I went over the concept of how intelligent pigs really are. After the segment was over, the deal was that the pig would go back to the farmer. However, as I said earlier, once you spend a night with a pig, it's yours. Consequently, I brought the pig back to Long Island, where, however unreasonably, it is against the law to own a pig. I said to Fay, as if she didn't already know, "Spotty is our pig, and he is going to stay our pig." Mind you, I already owned a pig named Corky. So this was illegal pig number two. "It was amazing to get away with one, but," I kept saying to myself, "how am I going to get away with two?" Then I decided that Spotty was going to be my trained pig. I started walking him up and down the street, taught him how to walk on a harness lead, how to skateboard. People would look at Spotty and say, "hey, what's that?" And I would say, "Oh, it's a rare dog from Hungary, or Afghanistan." And they believed me, until Spotty got bigger and bigger, 120, 140, 160, 1,000 pounds—even New Yorkers thought it was strange. People started *squealing* on us, "Hey, that's a pig living on Long Island." We caved in to the pressure and began looking for a farm in upstate New York.

So, Dave and I became friendly, and after doing the show nearly a dozen times, the people at NBC became very familiar with me and my work. One segment I recall doing on the Letterman show was called the "Suit of Suet." In fact, that was one of the most classic segments we pulled off together. This was where we dressed Dave in a full-length bodysuit of suet—yes, suet: fat, seeds, ground-up carrots, and other goodies. He was just a human smorgasbord. The concept of the bit was to put Dave in a cage and surround him with different types of animals that would eat him. He thought it would be a funny idea and his producers agreed. It was NBC's job to create the suit of suet; my job was to supply the man-eating animals. Accordingly, I rounded up some deer, a llama, a goat, a squirrel, a raccoon, some birds, chickens, ducks, and geese—a whole variety of barnyard animals. It was Mother Goose revisited.

Dan Bleier, the props guy, concocted the suit of suet the night before the segment, and kept it in the refrigerator at the NBC commissary overnight to keep it cool and to keep it from rotting. (Jeez, I don't know if anyone will eat at that NBC commissary again.) It was an off-camera segment, meaning that I wasn't actually appearing on the show; I was keeping the animals together for the big feast. The idea was very simple. Dave would get into the cage dressed from head to toe in the suit of suet, and the animals would chow down on David Letterman—no big deal, right? As can be expected, the segment didn't come off as planned. There was something about that NBC commissary that wasn't kosher, because, as all the animals surrounded the cage with Dave cloaked in the suit of suet, not one animal took a nibble. It was as if they gave up suet for Lent.

Another classic Letterman story occurred on Canada Day. To commemorate the holiday, the producers decided to have a sled-dog race down the halls of NBC. Sled-dog race, halls of NBC, no snow—how are we going to get the response, how are we going to get the dogs to do this stunt? Call the Amazing Warren! Well, it was yet another miracle I pulled out of my hat. Straight to my Rolodex under "S." Sled dogs. Easy. I put together two teams of huskies. Dave on one team, and Paul Shaffer—a native Canuck—on the other team. Basically, the magic ingredient was wax. We waxed the floors real well, and waxed the sleds well, and we had this incredible race down the hallways of NBC. It went off without a hitch! The husky race was definitely a "classic" and is still talked about today.

Through the years, Dave and I forged a close relationship, and it was this relationship that really started me doing TV. Besides his morning show, one of the first TV shows I did was "The Tonight Show" with Dave as the guest host. I received his call back in New York: "Hey, Warren, I'm guest hosting 'The Tonight Show' and we want to bring you on to do a segment with my dogs, Bob and Stan. We'll do it on anything you want." At that time, Fay and I had just finished writing our second book, *Pet Aerobics: An Exercise Book for Dogs and Cats*, so we decided to do puppy push-ups and doggy sit-ups on "The Tonight Show."

Fay and I then flew out to California. It was our first trip anywhere since we had been married, more than ten years earlier—our work schedules made it impossible. In any case, we decided that even though the "Tonight Show" was going to put us up, we were going to upgrade ourselves to the Beverly Hills Hotel. "Here we are in California, we might as well live it up. Who knows if we'll ever be back?"

I remember going to the NBC Studios in Burbank, and let me tell you, I was catatonic for two weeks before we did this segment. I was paralyzed with fear. I mean, this was national television, "The Tonight Show." I used to eat dinner with Johnny Carson every night because I'd just be getting home from work at 11:30 P.M., when he was going on the air.

We did the segment, and while it was funny, it wasn't the most successful one I ever did, I've got to be honest with you. It was probably too ambitious to do pet aerobics while there was so much noise and distraction in the studio. However, I do remember one comment Dave made that was very humorous. No matter what I did, the dogs kept pulling toward Doc Severinsen and the band. Dave turned to me and said, "Warren, obviously you trained the dogs to sniff contraband."

I was completely starstruck by one of Dave's guests that night: Lily Tomlin. When I went back to the dressing room after the show feeling a little low, there was actually a note from Lily asking to see me.

The Story of Tess

After the show, an NBC page came running over to my dressing room. "Warren, Ms. Tomlin would like to see you," she said. Apparently Ms. Tomlin wasn't leaving anything to chance, so I went to see her in her dressing room. There she was, surrounded by a group of people with strange-colored hair and her Norwich terrier, who seemed overly timid and shy—even a little snappy. Lily commented, "You know, Warren, I'm having some problems with

Tess, perhaps you can help me out." We spoke for a little while there, and then we made an agreement that the next time I was in

Lily Tomlin and her Norwich terrier Tess—they shared (all) the same personalities.

the Los Angeles area, I would help her resolve some of the problems Tess was exhibiting.

The first time I pulled up to her house I was stunned. She lived on the old W. C. Fields estate, painted pink. There was this enormous gate around the front. I talked to the intercom and the gate swung open, revealing a long drive up to the house, with a 1940s Mercury convertible parked in front. After Lily and her staff greeted me warmly, I had a sense of déjà vu—many of the mansion's furnishings were from the set of *The Incredible Shrinking Woman*. One of the tables in the living room was the oversized cassette recorder used in the movie to make her seem smaller. Out by the pool, she had the rocking chair from "Laugh In." I must have seemed pretty wide-eyed—my drooling must have given me away.

It was to become an ongoing relationship, and working with Lily and her staff was truly gratifying. They were like neighbors, just incredibly nice, down-to-earth people. And let's face it, Tess was a mess!

Working with Tess was a unique challenge—she was "Sybil" of the canine world! This dog had multiple personalities. She could be your best friend for an hour, then suddenly, for no reason, she would turn around and give you a little snap.

Meanwhile, I observed Lily practicing several different personalities every day. One minute she's Ernestine, the telephone operator; the next she's a little girl licking a giant sucker. Tess was dealing with twenty different owners, and as a result, the dog was a little insecure and confused.

"Lily," I said, "the dog hasn't a problem. She just doesn't know who she lives with. Just put Ernestine and the others into the closet for at least fifteen minutes each day and be yourself. Just Lily." I suggested she also strengthen that bond by taking Tess for a walk or a jog every day. After many, many months of therapy, we were able to work things out.

Another problem was that because Tess traveled with Lily all over the country, we needed to develop a routine to keep her in shape. The dog's tummy was getting close to the ground, so I taught her to do wind sprints on hotel staircases.

Tess lived a long and happy life with her best friend. I recall visiting Lily backstage during her one-woman Broadway show, *Signs of Intelligent Life*, and, of course, Tess was backstage, too. Lily also had a goat named Bucky that Fay and I had worked with and there was also a cat. At one point, Cheryl, Lily's assistant, even sent her Blue Doberman, Diva, from L.A. to New York, where she spent a few months training with me.

You'd never expect a celebrity of Lily's immense talent and stature to be so unassuming, but having worked and spent time with her, I found her to be extraordinarily unpretentious and unbelievably kind.

On one trip out to the West Coast, Fay went into what is called ketoacidosis and almost died. I had Tige, the Buster Brown dog, with me at the time. We had just checked into the Beverly Wilshire Hotel, and all of a sudden Fay said she wasn't feeling well. Fay, who was not a complainer, then said she felt dizzy and was going to pass out. I quickly called the front desk to find the closest hospital. It turned out to be Century City Hospital, which was down the street. I took her over there and, unbelievably, the doctor told me he didn't know if she was going to survive. It came on that fast.

Unbeknownst to me, the hospital had an outstanding diabetic ward and Fay was treated by Mary Tyler Moore's physician. She spent almost a full week there in intensive care. I was commuting back and forth to the hotel to walk Tige. The dog and I pretty much lived on hash browns and scrambled eggs for the entire week. I would order one for myself and one for him. During this trying time, Lily sent flowers and called constantly. Her concern made a major difference in Fay's recovery, so far from our home and family.

Little did I know that if I ever made it to the Emmys, I'd be dressed up like a chauffeur and have a Russian wolfhound in each hand.

One of the most exciting times in my life was accompanying Lily to the 1984 Emmy Awards in Pasadena. Actually, "accompanying her" is kind of an understated way of putting it. She had decided she was going to the Emmys dressed as Ernestine—Ernestine as an art deco–esque kind of person with two art deco–esque dogs. So I suggested twin Russian wolfhounds—the dogs from the vodka commercials. Accordingly, I flew out to California and Lily decided that I would dress up in a 1920s' chauffeur's uniform, with spats. I got out of the car at the Emmy Awards dressed in the chauffeur's costume—I don't know where I got the guts to do this—and walked these two Russian wolfhounds around the car and handed them to Lily, who was dressed as Ernestine. So up went Ernestine to do her thing. It was quite dazzling to be a player caught up in this Hollywood night, and see how well orchestrated this whole event is. The attention she drew sashaying up, dressed as Ernestine accompanied by these two dogs was amazing, and she sent me a really nice card after that. It was truly a memorable occasion.

The Fred Wilpon Story

After many years, I was becoming the trainer most in demand with that part of the population considered the "A" List. I was getting loads of calls from all the affluent areas of Long Island—Sands Point, Kings Point, Roslyn, Brookville, Old Westbury, and Great Neck. Coming from a very blue-collar household, I was blown away whenever I went into these houses. These were mansions, estates, maybe even home to *millionaires*! And occasionally, I would run into a problem. Here's a perfect example: I was training a dog for Fred Wilpon, who was one of the owners of the New York Mets. He had a golden retriever puppy and was referred to me through the horse show circuit. I had gone to their home in the exclusive area of Roslyn Harbor on the north shore of Long Island and met with Mrs. Wilpon. Over a period of months, I worked with the dog and then worked with both Mrs. Wilpon and their son in teaching the dog the basic commands. He pretty much mastered the heel, sit, come, stay, and off-leash work. The dog was still young and had a lot of energy, and for the most part, he responded successfully about 85 percent of the time, which is really all that should be expected. I wish most *people* would respond at that level! In any case, I arrived at the house for one of the final meetings with the dog, and as I walked in there was Mr. Wilpon. Now, Mr. Wilpon was never present at any of our training sessions, but all of a sudden the man just started yelling at me. "This dog doesn't listen to me . . . is this how you built your reputation?"

And I responded, "Perhaps if you were involved in the training of the dog, then the dog would be more responsive to you."

"Well, that's why I hired you," he said. That's like hiring someone to exercise for you—it just doesn't work. I asked Mrs. Wilpon if the dog responded to her and she said yes and the son agreed, too. So I said, "There's the answer: The dog also responds well to me; it seems like you are the only one to whom the dog does not listen. And you are the only one who is not working with the dog."

He then yelled, "Let's take this outside."

I thought to myself, where are we heading here?

He took me outside. "You'll listen to me and you'll do what I tell you to do, because I have more money than you and I'll put an ad in the newspaper saying that you are a lousy dog trainer."

I turned to him. "You know," I said, "I don't know who has more money than who. [I had about a nickel to my name.] The dog is trained. The dog responds to me, your wife, and your son. You are the only one the dog does not respond to and that is because you could give a shit about your dog just like you give a shit about everything else." Mr. Wilpon backed off and walked into the house, and that was the last I heard from him.

The bottom line is that if you designate only one person in the home to work with the trainer, then the dog is going to respond to only *that* person. *It's up to everyone else in the home to then carry out the training in the same fashion.* And if one person tells the dog to get up and another tells the dog to get down, then you're going to have one neurotic little puppy. It was a classic example of problems that can occur in training, but more important, it best exemplifies the asinine attitude that just because they have a lot of money, some people think they can force their dog to listen to them.

At this point I was working with a lot of sports figures. I had never been to a hockey game in my life, nor had I even seen a hockey game on TV, but all of a sudden I was the dog trainer to the New York Islanders. At that time, the team was unstoppable and had won the Stanley Cup year after year after year. Basically, my attorney at the time—who incorporated Master Dog Training but was later indicted and lost her license—was a big Islanders fan and a big booster. She would go to Islander booster parties, and when the subject of pets and dogs came up, she'd refer them to me. The first Islanders dog I trained was for Clark Gillies. He had a reputation for starting fights on the rink. He was one of those guys who, whenever there was a brawl, would be right there in the middle! In any case, I worked with his dog Hombre—a German shepherd mix—and his wife. If I remember correctly, Hombre had a bad chewing problem, which we went on to resolve. I even had one of my trainers work with Hombre.

After Clark Gillies, it seemed like I was getting a call from another player every day. I trained the dogs of Jude Drouin and Chico Resch, who, in turn, referred me to Bryan Trottier. I drove out to his house in East Northport, Long Island, where Bryan introduced me to his cocker spaniel, Patrick Henry. I think every player had a dog, and they all had problems with them. I ultimately did go to see a hockey game. And what amazed me most about these guys was the contrast between their actions on and off the ice. During the games, these guys were maniacs. I mean, if you just looked at a player the wrong way, you would get yourself knocked over the head with a hockey stick or punched in the stomach. Interacting with their dogs, they were so incredibly gentle. It was a fun time for me because people would come up to me and say, "Oh, you know Jude Drouin and Bryan Trottier." I was a hero just for knowing these guys. I guess to New York hockey fans, working with these guys was a really big thing.

Once I was working with the Islanders, all the other New York teams followed. I got a call from one of the biggest players I had ever met: Marty Lyons of the New York Jets; followed by Clark Gaines, a running back, and then Pat Ryan, a quarterback. They just kept coming in one after another. I became friends with these guys and I even went fishing with Clark, though we never caught anything. It just floored me how these players were killers on the field, but so incredibly sweet with their pets.

It was also the time when the Mets were in the playoffs, and I got a call from Lenny Dykstra, who was probably one of the hottest players at the time. I went to his house to teach his wife some basic commands for their German shepherd, which is when it dawned on me that all the ballplayers were married to nearly identical, tall, blond, model-type women. It was also incredible how all the players used the same lawyers, doctors, and accountants. I guess I was lucky to become the animal shrink to the sports stars!

Mrs. Woolworth and More

This marked the time when I began doing a lot of training on Park and Fifth avenues. All of a sudden, for whatever reason, I started getting lots of calls from extremely affluent people. Some of them were great and some were difficult—to say the least. One of the most fascinating was Mrs. Woolworth. (Yes, *the* Mrs. Woolworth.) She lived on Park Avenue, but I still showed up dressed in an army fatigue shirt, ripped jeans, and with my hair pulled back in a ponytail. The doorman sighed with a disgusted look and said, "Who are you?"—as if I were a homeless person stumbling inside. Against his better judgment he buzzed up and the staff said, "Oh yes, Mr. Eckstein, send him up!" It sort of shocked the doorman.

On my first visit, I took the elevator all the way up to the top floor. When I got off, there were no other doors, just this long hallway leading to Mrs. Woolworth's apartment. I knocked on the door and this finely appointed butler answered. This guy was straight out of *Sunset Boulevard*. He invited me to sit down in the parlor, and said, "Mrs. Woolworth will be right with you." Sure enough she came right out, dressed impeccably, as though she were serving high tea, and even wore white gloves. I remember thinking to myself, "I'm in a Bette Davis movie." It was just that kind of feeling. Anyway, she wanted basic training for her small dog—a cocker spaniel, I believe—which we proceeded to do over the course of the next few months. Surprisingly, she took a very "hands on" approach to the training and was fun to work with. She was pleased with the results and became just another happy client in the Eckstein "Who's Who" of referrals. She was a savvy businesswoman, too. When I quoted her the price for training her dog, she bickered with me on the amount. I didn't cave in to her pressure, however. "That is my price and if I went any lower that means I lied to you at first," I told her.

And she replied, "You're going to go somewhere son, you're going to go somewhere." Mrs. Woolworth was an amiable lady, and I enjoyed working with her dog. Improving the dog's manners also elevated my relationship with the doorman, who eventually greeted me like a family member!

From Park Avenue, it was a short hop over to Fifth Avenue. I got a call from a woman who worked for a Mrs. Sulzberger, a member of the family that owned the *New York Times*. She owned a little papillon with some French name like Pierre. These Fifth Avenue apartments were truly incredible; constructed as duplexes, they were actually preservation sites in old historic buildings in the wealthiest part of town. It was truly fascinating for me coming from a split level on Long Island. These experiences were a high. I don't believe I really appreciated it then, but I do now! Mrs. Sulzberger was an elderly woman, but quite agile and spry. She frequented the ballet, the opera, and other cultural events. Her papillon played a pivotal role in her life, and she wanted some basic training. We started the training process, and on the second meeting we talked about specific training.

Mrs. Sulzberger said to me, "Warren, you know how I keep in shape?"

"No," I replied. "How do you keep in shape?"

"Well, I dance every morning, and I would really like it if Pierre could be taught to get up on his hind legs and dance with me." I remember laughing to myself, but then I thought, "Who am I to laugh? The lady wants to dance with her dog." I even recalled seeing Fay pick up the front paws of our dog and dance around many a time, and we would later devote an entire chapter to dancing in our 1984 book *Pet Aerobics*. So I rethought it: good exercise for her; good exercise for the dog. However, being as shy as I am (though sometimes I know it's hard to tell), I was reluctant to have an audience, so I said to her, "Well, I can't do that in front of you. You are going to have to go in the other room and I'll have to work with the dog by myself." So Pierre and I worked on dancing for a couple of weeks. Now, this was no disco dog; I simply observed his natural movements and, bearing in mind who his owner was, opted for ballroom dancing. One two, one-two-three—taking three little steps in place over and over again, we learned the cha-cha. Pierre turned into a real hoofer and Mrs. Sulzberger was delighted when her companion papillon accompanied her in dancing and exercising every day, and lived happily ever after. Pierre was a great little dog, but what is more important, he was an impressive lead and did a mean cha-cha!

From Park Avenue and Fifth Avenue, I ventured right to the entrance of the Carlyle Hotel. I'll never forget this job; it was fun, interesting, and informative. I received a call to see a couple whose last name was Petrie. They lived in the penthouse apartment at the Carlyle Hotel at the corner of Madison and Seventy-sixth. The Carlyle is one of the most famous hotels in New York. That was where Bobby Short played the piano, and that was where the famous Bemelman bar is located with all the murals by Ludwig Bemelman adorning the walls. Not being a society person, I had no idea who the Petries were, or what status the name carried. It turns out that Milton Petrie and his wife, Carol, whom I believe was once married to a count, were among the wealthiest people in the country as well as famed philanthropists. I recall being told that Mrs. Petrie actually bought a house in the Hamptons for her husband without even seeing it. Milton Petrie was an elderly man who continued to work every day. I only worked with him once or twice, but he was a fascinating gentleman, and a real study of New York society.

The Petries had two dogs: a shar-pei, which I worked with, and a one-eyed Boston terrier named Begin, after the Israeli prime minister. I thought the name was pretty odd, but walking around the apartment I saw autographed pictures of Menachem Begin, Mother Teresa, and several U.S. presidents. The only thing that bothered me, as I sat in the living room in awe of the incredible view of the city, was their souvenir from a safari: two elephant tusks. Such trophy hunting was offensive to me, but it wasn't for me to raise their consciousness. I went on to do my job, which lasted twelve or thirteen weeks. I was in one of those situations where the dog was incredibly bright and the owners were incredibly bright, but their schedules did not allow them to practice the training with the dog. Consequently, I was left to work with one of the maids who was supposed to follow through on the training and walk the dog, so it really never received the proper attention. Despite these obstacles, the dog came out wonderfully and actually appeared with me on "The Today Show," where I talked about pet psychology.

The colorful part of this experience was the education *I* received in addition to training the Petries' pet. I would visit the Carlyle once or twice a week. Generally, I would have several clients in the city and I would line them all up together. Occasionally, however, I would have an hour between jobs and, not being too familiar with the city, I started frequenting Bemelman's. Although I would not classify myself as a drinker, I would have a glass of white wine or a beer, and I befriended the bartender. He had some classic stories to tell. I was probably the only person asking for a Pabst Blue Ribbon. Most people ordered martinis and other high-class drinks. I have to admit I was intimidated by these wealthy people, but I never let my feelings impede my ability to train the dog.

After completing their dog's training, Mrs. Petrie told me that one of her neighbors wanted to speak with me. We took the elevator down a couple floors and now I was walking into another beautiful apartment, which was occupied by Patty Davis, the daughter of Marvin Davis—owner of Twentieth Century-Fox. We chatted and I gave her some advice for her dog. Her schedule required that she travel a lot, so nothing ever came of our meeting. Still, it was pretty interesting sitting around with the rich and the famous. One thing I have discovered over the years: When it comes to pets, it doesn't matter how much money you have, or how much money you don't have. Pets are the great equalizers.

It was intriguing to see the path my life had taken. I went from training all the dogs for the wise guys, to becoming the dog psychologist and behaviorist for the rich and famous.

I even received a call from Jacqueline Kennedy Onassis's sister Lee Radziwill. I went to her apartment for a preliminary meeting. At the time, she was dating a guy who seemed to think he was very important. The two things that come to mind when I think about this guy was that he was short and I didn't like him. The private training end of my business was getting really busy, so I was unable to personally train the Radziwill dog. The boyfriend's response, when I told him that "I really didn't have the time to do it thoroughly, but I would send one of my best-qualified trainers to work with the dog," was "Do you know who I am? Do you know who she is? You will train our dog!"

At that point I left the apartment. I called him the next day to

Some may go to the Playboy Mansion to see beautiful women; I chose to feed the monkeys.

let him know we would not be doing business together. He offered more money, and I simply told him I did not have the time. I missed my chance to forge a close bond with the extended family of the Kennedys!

Not long after the Radziwill call, I was contacted by a woman named Diahn Williams. She was probably the first person I ever met named Diahn. She was an actress and she owned an estate in Lloyd Harbor on Long Island, along with her husband Tom McGrath, an attorney. They wanted me to come and take a look at their German shepherd, Shamus (which was a big movie at the time). As I drove out to their address in Lloyd Neck I passed the estates of some renowned individuals, including Billy Joel. Just to give you an idea of the level of these people: There was an argument going on regarding an Arab sheik who was landing his helicopter on his lawn; the neighbors were not too thrilled about it. Anyway, I went to meet with Diahn and her servant Maria. This estate was so grandiose it had its own name: Pepperhill Farm. I entered the gates and drove, and drove, and drove. I continued up the curvy road until I finally made my way to the moat. (Yes, there was an actual body of water surrounding the house.) The estate more closely resembled a castle than a mansion. And the previous owners had been the Fairchilds. The manor rested on a cliff overlooking the beautiful Long Island Sound. The training with the shepherd went very smoothly. He was excellent for me and worked well with Diahn, but again my gut reaction was that once we were finished the dog would be left in the hands of the maid.

Through the training process, Diahn and I became good friends. And actually, that's probably where I caught the bug for doing some TV, because after we became friendly, we chatted about the vagaries of my career, which intrigued her. She even wanted to write a movie about my life, about the people I've worked with and what I had been doing with myself and the animals up until that point. So we started writing *My Life* and it was called *Chester and Adam*. We wrote the entire script and she even had it registered with the Writers Guild of America.

At the time, Diahn and her husband were producing a movie. She was the star and her costars were Don Murray, James Earl Jones, Treat Williams (in his first movie), and Lillia Scalla, a two-time Academy Award winner. Interestingly enough, the director of the movie was a man by the name of Ivan Nagy, who became the focus of a lot of attention in 1994 because of his involvement with Heidi Fleiss, the convicted "Hollywood Madam." I was not particularly fond of Mr. Nagy when I first met him. They had contacted me to work with a dog for the movie. Specifically, there were a couple of places during the movie where the German shepherd belonging to Lillia Scalla had to carry a newspaper or bark a couple of times on cue. While the dog was not to be used often, I still had to be on the set frequently, because they didn't know when they would need the dog. I decided to use my mom's dog, Smokey. Several months earlier I had found Smokey, thin and battered, as a stray on the street, and since then she had become one of the most loving and responsive dogs I had ever worked with.

It was going to be a difficult movie to make as it was to be filmed on location, and it would take a special dog to remain calm with the confusion of people, lights, cameras, and wires. Yet Smokey performed so magnificently and easily that she surprised everyone. Out of hundreds of retakes, only one was due to her error. This one occasion called for Smokey to bark, and the dog was just not in a barking mood. Impatiently, Ivan Nagy gestured and then said, "Well, just *kick the dog* to get her to bark."

I turned to him angrily and said, "Before the dog gets kicked, I'll kick you. The dog will bark when she wants to bark." From then on, I knew there was something about this guy that I did not find the least charming.

In the end, the movie was not a huge success, but it has aired several times on television. It's fun to go back and watch it and see how it was all put together. My relationship with Diahn was interesting because it lasted a good couple of years. I not only trained her dog, but we met weekly to work on the *Chester and Adam* script, which was completed and since then was passed over, probably for *Ishtar*. It was never made into a movie but, as things turn out, maybe it makes a better *book!*

Cheryl Tiegs

In among a stack of phone messages I picked up at the office one day was one from Tony Peck, with no other information. We always knew where the calls were coming from, whether it was a New York City call or Long Island call, by the area code. We played phone tag for a while—I would leave messages with a foreign-speaking maid. He in turn left messages for me, and he sounded very important. However, other than Gregory Peck, the name Peck meant nothing to me. Finally we connected, and it turned out that he and his girlfriend were referred to me by some friends. They had a wirehaired fox terrier that needed basic training and he wanted me to come and evaluate the dog, then quote him a price. We were to meet at their apartment on Park Avenue. We set up an appointment and I ventured out to meet the couple and their dog. Their apartment was located in this beautiful, historic building. As I walked up, I was greeted (?) by a doorman dressed in tails and white gloves. I, of course, was wearing ripped blue jeans, long hair, and my staple army fatigue T-shirt. The doorman informed me that I would need to use the service elevator. I smiled and simply told him that I was there to evaluate Mr. Peck's dog, and could he buzz up. Once again I made it past the doorman and went up to Mr. Peck's apartment. I walked in and met the young Tony Peck. While we were making our introductions, in swept this impossibly gorgeous blonde. The impact of her beauty took my breath away! I managed to make eye contact with her, and while she looked familiar, I couldn't place her—I wasn't a big TV watcher or magazine reader at the time—hey, I was working a hundred hours a week. Tony then introduced us: "Warren, this is Cheryl Tiegs. Cheryl, this is Warren." Ahh, the name finally clicked and I was flabbergasted. There I was with Tony Peck (Gregory Peck's son, although I didn't know it at the time) and Cheryl Tiegs in this stunning duplex apartment on Park Avenue with their adorable wirehaired terrier puppy, Martini. I quoted them a price and looked at the dog. It was an incredible animal and we decided that I'd give some of the lessons at the apartment on Park Avenue and some training at Cheryl's house on Montauk

Point, a rather exclusive area on Long Island. In addition, there would be some brush-up lessons at their West Coast home, because I was already heading out there monthly for my media commitments.

It was a pleasure to train Martini because he was such a bright dog. I can always tell what a person is all about by the personality of their pet. Cheryl's dog had her personality—very bubbly and outgoing. If he had been blond and had blue eyes, Martini would be a model! I worked with the dog in the apartment and on the streets of New York City with Cheryl and Tony. Tony was doing a movie at the time—I believe it was *Brenda Starr* with Brooke Shields. Then he was making another movie, *Pirates*, which was being filmed in Tunisia. Cheryl would travel to Tunisia to visit Tony and the only person she would leave Martini with was me! I remember being at home in Oceanside when their stretch Rolls-Royce pulled up to my little Cape Cod house. All my neighbors were peering out of their windows watching the chauffeur open the doors and, to everyone's surprise, grasp the leash as Martini trotted out.

Cheryl would fly back and forth to the West Coast, and there were times when I would meet her in California. I would be flying coach on TWA and the dog would be flying first class on MGM Grand Air. I had a great time working with Martini and Cheryl. We all became relatively good friends. Fay would occasionally come out with me to train the dog at Montauk Point and it was just an enjoyable time for everyone. I remember arriving at 8:30–9:00 A.M. and knocking on the door to no answer. We rang the bell and continued to knock on the door, but apparently she was still asleep. She came downstairs in a robe, her hair tousled, and *still* this lady was stunning! Not a drop of makeup and just out of bed, yet she looked ready to walk the runway—she was that attractive. More important, however, was the fact that Cheryl was so down to earth—"Warren, can I make you some coffee?" She always managed to put people at ease despite being one of the top models in the world.

As the training with Martini progressed, so did my friendship with Cheryl. Then they got a second dog, Olive. So now we had Martini and Olive, and I would joke with Cheryl, saying, "What are you going to call the next one: Swizzle Stick?" In any case, both dogs advanced very well with the training.

On one of my West Coast trips I had an appointment to work with Cheryl in Bel Air. It turned out that she was staying in the guest cottage at the estate of her by then father-in-law, Gregory Peck. This "cottage" was a place I could have retired to and lived out the rest of my life in. Anyway, I was working with the dogs on the deck by the pool, and out walked Gregory Peck. It was probably the one time I was so starstruck that I couldn't utter a word. I wasn't particularly a huge Gregory Peck fan, and I don't even think I could name one Gregory Peck movie, but he simply radiated the presence of a true legend. (You know what I mean.) He turned out to be a super guy. The Pecks had this beautiful three-legged golden retriever who would run all over their property. That should give you an indication as to what kind of people they were. Tony and Cheryl were equally kind and caring. When Fay became ill, Cheryl was really supportive. They were the kind of people who come into your life for a brief period of time, and although you may not see them, you always know somehow, somewhere, there was a bond. Like the time Cheryl had completed a big modeling job and had over a hundred pairs of shoes. She called Fay and asked for her size, offering her a choice of shoes. Well, Fay's foot wasn't the same size, but it showed the kind of consideration that makes me think so positively and so fondly of Cheryl Tiegs.

Geraldine Ferraro

One day, one of the staff called me to the phone saying that a politician wanted my services. Not being one who follows politics, the call didn't mean anything to me. But when I understood it was Geraldine, it meant the world to me. This was during the time she was the 1984 candidate for vice-president on the Mondale/Ferraro ticket, and was receiving a tremendous amount of press around the country as the first woman to run for vice-president.

As a result of her rigorous campaigning schedule, her beautiful German shepherd, Sammy, was suffering from separation anxiety, and was acting out by doing a lot of destructive chewing around the Ferraro household. After the call, I just had a good feeling that I would like her. I knew from reading about her and having watched her on television that she was a dynamic woman. I didn't know how I would feel about her kids, because kids can be entirely different from the parents. And after the bad press her husband had received and after watching him on television, I didn't think I would like John Zaccaro.

Well, I ventured out to their gorgeous home in Forest Hills, Queens, and John answered the door in a pair of preppie bermuda shorts. I walked inside and was introduced to both Geraldine and her daughter, and then to Sammy. I quickly came to the conclusion that Sammy was indeed suffering from separation anxiety. The dog had actually chewed up some needlepoint Geraldine was doing while she was on the campaign trail.

I spent several weeks working with the family, and to my surprise I really began to like John Zaccaro. He was a businessman, but he was a down-to-earth nice guy. It just goes to show that you cannot always believe what you read or see in the press. Although Geraldine's bid for vice-president proved unsuccessful, Sammy did improve, and life in the Zaccaro household went on. I greatly enjoyed working with Geraldine because she personified true class!

For years after the training was finished, I received several letters from Sammy (obviously written by Geraldine) to update me on the family. Geraldine would even take the time to put Sammy's paw print on every letter she sent. I said to myself, "Imagine this. Here we have the first woman to run for the office of vice-president taking the time to put her dog's paw on an ink pad, stamp the card, and then clean off the dog's paw just as a gesture of gratitude." She was and still is a fascinating woman, and she should have won the election!

TV AND
THEATER

"Saturday Night Live"

Dan Bleier, a good friend of mine, who, as prop master at "The David Letterman Show" worked with me in making arrangements for the animals, jumped ship and started working on the staff of "Saturday Night Live." It was his job to acquire any prop needed for the show, and a lot of their skits required animals. Hence, through my contact with Dan, I became the animal wrangler and resident trainer for "Saturday Night Live." It proved to be one of the most challenging jobs I'd ever have, but it was also one of the most fun. I got to meet some comedic giants like Robin Williams, Dana Carvey, and Jon Lovitz as well as the various people hosting and working on the cast in the late eighties. This was extremely strenuous, because the show was live and the days were long. We would generally go in Friday for a dress rehearsal and on Saturday we would be there from 10:00 A.M. until the show went off the air, fifteen hours later, at 1:00 A.M. For those who have never been behind the scenes, it is incredible to see how many people are involved in putting together a successful program like "SNL." There are wardrobe people who dress the stars, hairdressers, makeup artists; writers, producers, directors, catering people, and dozens of assistants—plus the actors. Then add the sizable entourages for the guest host and musical group. In any case, the show was demanding. Staying with a chicken or a pig in a closed room for eighteen hours can *really* clear your nose.

One of the most memorable episodes I did involved actress Glenn Close. This was truly one of the most difficult skits I ever tried to pull off in my television career. We wanted to do "Westminster Kennel Club Goes Bad." The writers' concept was that Glenn Close would play a dog show judge and have seven or eight dogs on the stand (where dogs would be when they were being judged). Glenn would go to examine the dogs and they would all turn and attack her! Then, through the miracle of television, she would be all bloody and ripped to shreds. This was very difficult because I had to use dogs that looked very aggressive; at the same time, I had to concern myself with the safety of Glenn Close. I remember hiding behind boxes all over the set to monitor the animals. Ultimately, I used Schutzhund-trained dogs, which was not an easy task, by the way. Schutzhund is a type of training done in Europe that is obedience tracking and protection. And it took several weeks to find seven dogs trained in that method. I spent a lot of time with them until we got to the point where the dogs would respond the way we wanted them to. At the time of the actual skit, Glenn Close would walk on and examine the dogs and they would act friendly. Then she would step just off-camera and I would appear and make a face to cue the dogs to growl and to show some teeth. The skit worked incredibly well, and I was truly proud of it.

Another skit involved Robin Williams and Jon Lovitz doing Shakespeare. Robin Williams was doing improv and Lovitz would get mad at him. This skit was challenging because we had chickens, ducks, and a pit bull sitting in the audience gazing on as Williams and Lovitz performed. Getting a chicken to sit peacefully next to a pit bull took a bit of work, but we got it done. Donkeys, rabbits, chickens, horses, turtles, ducks, among others were all frequent cast members on the show. Another aspect of the show that made it interesting was the fact that you never knew what was going to actually happen until the show went on the air. I remember getting there early in the morning and going through the rehearsals with the dogs. And I would do extra rehearsals by myself just to get the dogs adjusted to the set. Then we would do a second set of rehearsals, and then a dress rehearsal. Coincidentally, many people do not know that "Saturday Night Live" has two audiences: one for the dress rehearsal and another for the actual show. What is seen in dress rehearsal might be totally different from the actual broadcast.

For instance, one time we were doing a skit with Dana Carvey and Jon Lovitz playing two men sitting on a porch set in the Appalachian Mountains. To complete the picture, they needed some bloodhounds. In rehearsal, the bloodhounds worked perfectly, but one of the comedians complained that he was being upstaged by the dogs—saying he thought the audience would be looking at the dogs and not at him. Consequently, unbeknownst to me, when the final cut came, they did not use the dogs. If I remember right, without the hounds, the skit was a bust. We still got paid, though, and had a good time, and that was the bottom line.

Lorne Michaels was at every single "Saturday Night Live." I always remember him walking in with a bottle of white wine, which he put on his table while he sat there producing the show.

At this time in my career, a lot of things were happening for Fay and me. I was traveling a lot, doing promotional tours and book signings all over the country. Sometimes we would get calls to do "SNL" or "Letterman" when I wasn't available. If I was out of the state, Fay would handle it. There was 105-pound Fay doing incredible feats, like the time "SNL" wanted to do a "Pet Confessional." Dan called Fay, who reached me on the road (wherever I was at the time). The writers devised a skit in which they would have a priest and a confessional setup; the animals would go in and confess their sins to the priest. It was a very funny concept. A few hours later, Fay phoned to say that all the animals were booked and everything was ready to go. Then our office got a threatening call: "You are orchestrating a sacrilege on 'Saturday Night Live.' If you go through with it, your dog will be cut up and thrown out on your lawn." NBC received a threatening call as well. We had all the dogs there and had been through seventeen hours of rehearsal, when they decided to cut it at the last second. I don't know for sure if it was cut because the segment was not working well, or because of the death threats.

If I thought "Saturday Night Live" was a challenge, it was a vacation in paradise compared to what would unfold next in my life, and abruptly bring my era at "SNL" to a close.

Lions, Tigers, and Bears — Oh My!

Apparently, as a result of my appearances on "The Tonight Show" and "Late Night with David Letterman," I had generated some interest. I got a call in 1982 from a staffer at what was then Metromedia—Channel 5 in New York. The producer was in the process of putting together a weekend show called "Saturday Morning Live" with host (a blast from the past) Gene Rayburn from the "Match Game." It would be a magazine-type experiment in media, consisting of two hours of live television with a lifestyle format.

In the cast already was a cook, a garden expert, a fashion professional, and craft expert, and they figured they would also try a pet segment. The operative word here is *try*. The producer downplayed it, telling me that they would probably run one or two segments, but he didn't believe it would have the longevity that he anticipated for other areas of the show.

I decided my first segment for the show would be "Exercise with Your Pet." I did a rehearsal of the segment, sort of a runthrough to see how it would come together. I went down to the broadcast studios on West 63rd Street with my own dog—Tige, the Buster Brown dog. We did the segment on exercising, and it all came together perfectly. The producers were thrilled.

A week later they called to tell me the show was a "go" and that they wanted me to do one or possibly two segments. Back then, the pay was a mere $125 a week, and I was paying for the transportation of all the animals out of my pocket. So I did the first week, then a second, a third, and a fourth week. They continued to say they couldn't guarantee the longevity of the pet segments. Yet when the numbers started coming in, the pet segments were

Gene Rayburn was the first TV host I ever worked with. Boy, what an education I got. Both these homeless pets were adopted by staff.

receiving the highest rating for the whole two hours. The bottom line was "Saturday Morning Live" gave me some essential experience. It was fifteen minutes every Saturday morning and the cast became a true ensemble. I would play off the garden guy and the cook would play off the fashion lady. Fortunately, I had freedom of expression, and I was able to do all types of segments on the show. For example, my "Pet on the Couch" segment became a famous part of the show. I would bring on a family and their pet, and I would analyze the dynamics of the relationship between them. In one incident, an argument became so heated that a husband slapped his wife on the air. That's how hot some of the pet discussions became.

Then there were the embarrassing moments, and because the show was live, every one was caught while the camera rolled on, unmercifully. One day I had brought Tige on to demonstrate some basic obedience training with Gene Rayburn, and within the course of the training, Gene would try to distract Tige by getting on his hands and knees and calling to him. The concept was that I had put Tige in his "stay" command, so he wasn't supposed to move until I said, "OK." However, Tige was being trained for so many things that he used to get bored, and one of the tricks he had to perform at appearances was to take the hat off the Buster Brown character, so he just loved hats. During this segment, Gene wasn't wearing a hat, but he was down on his hands and knees, and Tige automatically knew that when someone was on all fours, he should go over and take the hat off. I guess whether or not they were wearing a hat was secondary. There was Gene saying, "Come here, Tige, Uncle Gene wants you." Out of the blue, Tige went over and actually nipped Gene Rayburn's ear! Gene started laughing along with everyone else. It was a very, very funny piece.

Another segment Gene and I did involved babies and unusual animals. I had on the set a fallow deer, a llama, a goat, and a baby bear while I answered questions from the studio audience. With the cameras rolling and the llama behind me, all of a sudden I started feeling a little damp. The llama had just peed all over me. I mean, I was just drenched in llama urine and Gene started to laugh. Regardless, the show went on! I think "Saturday Morning Live" was really part of what built my reputation. The segments were much longer, a luxury compared to the two or three minutes that most TV shows generally slot for animal segments. I also had the opportunity to try a lot of different things with animals, and in the process, help a lot of people realize that animals really are people, too. It was the first time anyone had spoken of animals having emotions.

For one Saturday, I decided to do a studio spot on demonstrating the Heimlich maneuver, the "hug of life," for dogs. One of the ways to accomplish this is by straddling the dog, putting your hands under the rib cage, and lifting up, thereby freeing anything caught in the dog's throat. To demonstrate, I booked an Irish wolfhound—the largest breed of dog—thinking only of how it would be a very photogenic thing for the audience to see. I remember straddling the dog, but as I lifted up on its chest, the back of the dog hit me right on the groin. The camera cut away to host Bill Boggs just breaking up, along with the entire audience, and the laughs roared on for three or four minutes while I danced around the crew and the stage, doubled over with a much higher voice!

Some of my famous guests were alligators, and even elephants. A trademark of the segments was that any animal that appeared on the show would receive a hug and kiss from me, because that's just what I do. My reputation for hugs and kisses grew directly from "Saturday Morning Live." The show continued on for about

My weekly segments on Channel 5 in New York in the eighties. Notice how uncomfortable I looked. That changed as soon as I brought out the pets.

five years. Every Saturday morning, fifty-two weeks a year, non-stop, I had to create a different animal segment. In all honesty, this was an excellent training ground for what I needed to do. Simply tracking down hundreds of animals like llamas, deers, goats, lions, tigers, and bears was imperative in my learning where to find these animals on a moment's notice, transport them, and then work with them in the media.

Other television shows continued to provide more embarrassing moments. I was doing "The CBS Morning Program," hosted by Mariette Hartley and Roland Smith, with a segment on trendsetting pets that included a peacock, a mallard duck, and two goats. One of the goats belonged to a 4-H kid, and it was named Doody-Head. I was sitting outside by the Green Room having a conversation with Dave Barry, the humorist and author, about what I was doing on my segment. He was on-camera just before me. Suddenly Doody-Head decided to relieve himself, and there was no sidestepping it. Dave had to walk in goat poop in order to get to the set. The next day he mentioned the incident in his column. Another colorful TV moment in my career!

Then there was the segment on "Live at 5" on WNBC-TV in New York with anchorwoman Sue Simmons and a handful of puppies. She picked up one of the puppies, whose paw got caught in her blouse and kind of exposed her bra on-camera. It was quite funny, and during the commercial, she hurriedly rebuttoned herself. Another time, on "Weekend Today in New York," a show I do weekly, I was working with a twelve- or thirteen-foot-long python while explaining how mellow and relaxing snakes can be. I had the snake over my shoulder and was talking to reporter McGee

Hickey when the hot lights started heating up this reptile, which is always a problem with reptiles on the set. He kept squeezing and squeezing me, tighter and tighter. I've had snakes on me millions of times, but this one was wrapped around my chest and my neck. He was actually squeezing the wind out of me as I was doing the segment! After we walked off the set, we took the snake off and everything was fine, but my producer Kim Gerbasi laughingly re-

The Guru of Gossip—Cindy Adams! I had to teach her that just because it's furry doesn't mean you have to *wear* it!

marked, "Good show, Warren, but you were a little hard to understand toward the end—your voice kept getting higher and higher."

New York Post columnist Cindy Adams is also a regular on "Weekend Today in New York," and I have a lot of fun with her. She always pops in to see what animals I've brought in for the show, then writes about it in her column:

> Pet expert Warren Eckstein carts assorted creatures to his weekly Channel 4 "Saturday in New York" gigs. So I wander into his dressing room, expecting a fluffy huggy puppy. A large, long, unstunning lizard blinks at me. This was a real ugly. Didn't match my shoes or anything. And he/she/it is alone, all alone, like totally alone. No Eckstein, no keeper, no nobody. Not caged in, locked away or chained up. We're talking just plain lying there flat out on a table chilling out. A large, long, live lizard.
>
> Only in New York, kids, only in New York.

Biting Off More Than I Could Chew

I always adored working with reptiles. Ever since I was a boy, I was considered the proverbial kid in the neighborhood who not only had puppies and kittens but had every variety of snake. There is something about reptiles that truly amazes me! Yet a lot of people have phobias about them and other reptiles, something I could never understand. I have come to the conclusion that, in our Judeo/Christian society, where Bible stories going back to Adam and Eve are so strong, the snake always represents evil. Adding to this is the concept that snakes slither along the ground, without legs. And they don't have eyelids. (It is scientifically impossible to prove whether a snake is sleeping, because their eyes are always open.) They flick their tongues and, contrary to popular belief, the tongue is not the part where the venom would be if it were a venomous snake.

Over the years, I have had the opportunity of working with some gorgeous snakes, many of which are poisonous. For one segment on the "Saturday Morning Live" program in New York, we had to get all types of approval from the City of New York to the Mayor's Office. They even mandated that we have a standby doctor on the set with antivenin in case I was bitten. The segment was on the "World's Most Deadly Snakes," which involved such poisonous snakes as a rattlesnake, a king cobra, and a gaboon viper.

The gaboon viper, which inhabits rain forests and adjacent woodlands in much of Central Africa, has the longest fangs of any snake. It also has both hemotoxin and neurotoxin venoms, which is rare among snakes and is almost always lethal to humans. Having handled these animals, I know it is just a matter of having no fear and cupping them in the right way. But sometimes a bite does happen. As a matter of fact, the one snake that bit and almost killed Marlin Perkins of "Wild Kingdom" fame was the same gaboon viper that I was handling. An important thing to remember when handling these reptiles is that the studios are kept quite cold and reptiles are cold-blooded animals. As soon as the studio spotlights warm them up, it triggers their feeding instinct: *time to eat!* Hence, you have to anticipate this and be wary of the snake's reaction to bright, hot lights.

There are, of course, occasional misunderstandings. One time I was working with a nonvenomous snake on a TV show and the snake—a reticulating python—actually took a nice bite out of my hand. I was doing two segments that day, and the segment prior to the snake involved handling rodents. Once the python smelled the mice and rats on my hands, I was food to him. So it wasn't the snake's fault, it was mine, but I did learn my lesson after that to always take a break and thoroughly wash my hands before handling the reptiles.

Probably one of the only snakes I would not handle on the set was the black mamba. This is an aggressive African snake that is extremely quick and has the capability to lunge up to four feet off the ground. In addition, it is a multiple bite snake, biting more than once, whereas most snakes bite once and stop.

It was very intriguing to watch the looks of hosts on the various shows and gauge their reactions, ranging from Gary Collins on "Hour Magazine" to Bill Boggs or Gene Rayburn on "Saturday Morning Live" to Steve Edwards on "Good Day L.A." to Regis Philbin and Kathie Lee Gifford on their show. Ironically, when I come to a TV show with dogs and cats—or miniature horses, goats, sheep—everybody circles around me, showering me with compliments. "Oh, we love you, Warren, we wish we had your job." Yet when I show up at the studio with snakes, I am treated like I have the plague—even my producer won't come near me.

I was doing some work in the San Francisco area for a music video. I don't recall the name of the group, but around that time—the early days of MTV—I used to get a lot of calls from production companies in need of animals to use in music videos. The video was to take place in a desert and they needed two rattlesnakes. They flew me to San Francisco to oversee the project. By that time, I had been stung by a scorpion, which was no big deal, and been bitten by a gila monster. I did suffer some effects from the gila monster, but, obviously, I survived. Whenever we are using poisonous animals such as rattlesnakes, I always inform the crew to keep quiet and refrain from making sharp or sudden movements. Well, sure enough, someone on the set made a quick movement. I was directly behind the snake, and it, in turn, got me in the arm. I had to have an antivenin shot, and it was one of the most painful experiences I've ever had in my life. There were some hallucinations at the same time, and I was in agonizing pain. My arm swelled up like a balloon, and I am just thankful that the antivenin was available. Other than that, reptiles are a whole lot of fun to work with. People are always fascinated by them and I think all of the phobias about snakes and other reptiles are basically a fear of the unknown.

Another incident occurred in San Francisco when I did a show called "Mac and Mutley." It was a weekly pet show that aired on KPIX Television. I believe it is still airing at different times; for a while it was on the Discovery Channel. It was one of those shows that bounced around and I was the animal behaviorist on the show. We would travel to different locations in and around northern California, talking about specific animals and how to correct any behavior problems they may have. For one segment we were discussing reptiles. I had shown snakes, and one of the animals I had on was a large monitor lizard. Monitor lizards can be aggressive, and if you are bitten, it can become infected pretty quickly because their mouths are full of bacteria. I had called a reptile

Here I am with one of my main squeezes.

expert and we planned to meet in Marin County to do a shot with his six-foot-long monitor lizard. I arrived at the location and there was this beat-up, old pickup truck and a guy covered head to toe with tattoos. In the back of the truck was a wooden coffin with holes cut into it. Not to be stupid, I introduced myself and said I was looking for "Puff," the monitor lizard, but what was the purpose of the coffin? He replied that that was how Puff traveled, because it was the easiest way to get the large monitor lizard from place to place. The guy then added that he had bought the coffin used. ("Hmmmm," I thought, "where does one buy a *used* coffin?" Well, he had bought the coffin from one of the airlines in order to transport his larger lizards.) Puff turned out to be an incredible lizard and the segment was quite a success. The funny part was the "used coffin."

Then there was a segment I did for Metromedia in New York involving lion cubs and capybaras, which are large, primarily aquatic rodents from South America. We made arrangements to pick up the lion cubs at the Brooklyn Zoo in Prospect Park. Today, it is a fine location, but at that time, it was situated in a poor neighborhood. In any case, I went down to the zoo and met with the zookeeper and the lion keeper in order to socialize myself with the cubs before they went on the show. The zookeeper showed me their cage, and right alongside them was the mother. Now, it doesn't take a brain surgeon to understand that if there are young lions around, and there is a mother, invading her territory and tampering with her young is going to make the mother react in an aggressive manner. So I asked the lion keeper to move the cubs to a location that was away from their mother so she wouldn't get upset. The new one contained a guillotine-type door that separated the mom's cage from the cubs' cage. He assured me there was no need to worry because it was shut down tight and locked. By law, when you go into a cage with animals, the cage behind you must be locked. Now, visualize this: I am in the zoo locked in a cage with two lion cubs. Even though these two were young, they were beating the heck out of me. Then, *all of sudden I saw the mother. The door that was allegedly locked by the lion keeper was starting to rise ... and the mother was peering under it!* At that point, I started yelling "Get me out of here!" and Fay, who was standing outside the cage, began to scream. The door closed again, and the mother was stuck between the cages. The zookeeper finally came around to unlock me—after what seemed like an hour. I immediately examined where the lion keeper was supposed to have locked the guillotine door, and found, to my horror, a couple of wire Baggie ties where there should have been a lock. I grabbed the lion keeper and I yelled and screamed and came very close to whacking him on the head. You can imagine my frustration. From that time on, anytime I was working with exotic animals, I always checked the locks myself.

I was doing a TV show in New York, and one of the animals I was bringing on with me was a coatimundi, a type of mongoose from South America that kills snakes and other animals with its extremely sharp teeth. I borrowed him from a game farm, where I was told that the coatimundi had been handled on a regular basis and he would be fine. What the keeper neglected to tell me was that the original owner also had dogs, and that the dogs had attacked the coatimundi. Consequently, the animal hated the sight or smell of any dog and would instinctively try to kill the dog if given the opportunity.

We were in the process of taping the show and I took the coatimundi back to my kennel to stay overnight and then pick him up the next day to finish taping. As I opened the cage to feed the coatimundi it slipped by me—and went straight for a dog I had at the kennel. I had lots of dogs staying there, but there was one specific dog, little old Lady, that was close by. Just before the coatimundi reached the dog, I grabbed the end of its tail and held on with every bit of strength I had. He was fighting me, and he swung around and bit me. I could not let go at that point, because if I did, Lady was dead. "It's either me or a death sentence for this unsuspecting dog," I said to myself. So I held the coatimundi by the tail and finally maneuvered him back into the large kennel I had prepared for him. I didn't even feel the bite as it occurred because the teeth were so sharp, but I looked down at my hand and my severed finger was barely hanging on. "OK, Warren," I said to myself, "you've taken worse bites than this!" Interestingly enough, the way my finger looked, I assumed it was gone. And if I was going to have a disability, then four fingers was not the worst. But there was blood all over the place; everything in the kennel was red. We put a towel around my finger and hand and ran over to the South Nassau Hospital in Oceanside.

At the hospital, the doctor asked me what had happened. I told him I was bit by a coatimundi. "What kind of dog is that?" he asked. I replied that it was like a mongoose. And he asked again, what kind of dog? He just couldn't quite understand what I was saying. I guess one wouldn't expect a patient to be bitten by a coatimundi in the middle of suburban Oceanside. I ended up getting about 100 stitches, but we still went on to do the show the next day—only I did it with a big bandage on my hand.

The ironic part of the story was that my best friend in the world, Warren DiCarlo—Deco—with whom I have been friends for more than twenty years, had recently suffered a similar accident involving a shark. Deco was an avid fisherman, and about a month before my coatimundi incident, he was participating in a shark-fishing tournament. He had caught a nice size shark, and in the process of bringing the shark out of the water and getting the hook out of its mouth, the shark took a bite out of Deco's finger. He was rushed to the hospital to have his finger sewed up and walked out with about fifty more stitches than he started with. Well, when I went to the hospital and my doctor heard me talking about being bitten by some exotic animal, he said to me, "You're not going to believe the guy who was in here about a month ago. He was bit by a shark and the shark wasn't even in the water!" Sure enough, he was talking about Deco; both of us stitched up by the same doctor.

"Hour Magazine"

Before "Saturday Morning Live" even ended, I got a call from Steve Clements in Los Angeles, who introduced himself as the executive producer for a nationally syndicated show called "Hour Magazine," hosted by Gary Collins. "We already have a pet expert on staff, but he's more of an author than a 'hands on' person. If we can find someone with the right chemistry for the show, we'll actually create an ongoing appearance every three to four weeks." Steve revealed that he'd seen a tape of me and Spotty appearing on the Letterman show and wanted me to fly in for an audition. "We'll send you a ticket; you'll do the show, and if we like it, we'll have you come back a couple times a year." Well, I went out to the studios and did a segment with Gary Collins—I forget who was cohosting at the time. After returning to New York, I told Fay: "I did the best I could; we'll see what happens." Sure enough, a week later Larry Ferber, their segment producer, called. He wanted me to do two segments so they could bank one to use later on. This is when my first national television exposure began, in the exclusive role "Hour Magazine" carved out for me as their regular pet and animal authority. From 1982 to 1988, I would fly out to California and tape two or three segments at a time. Steve Clements and I developed a close and enduring friendship, and over the years I had Gary Collins kiss just about every type of animal alive.

One day the cohosts were the entire cast of a popular television show at that time—"Head of the Class." I brought on a couple of large mastiffs, the 150-pound gentle giants of the dog world. While we were sitting there and talking about whatever the topic was, this horrific odor just overcame the stage and, obviously, wafted out into the audience. There was so much flatulence in the air that Gary's eyes started to tear as he looked at the cast from "Head of the Class," who, mortified, looked at me. I was looking at the audience unfazed, and the dogs just swayed in the breeze. Naturally, everyone blamed it on the dogs. To this day, I don't know who the real culprit was!

As embarrassing as these moments could be, I really believe it was these strange situations that created my career. It was the first time animals were ever shown on television as real living and breathing creatures. Prior to my appearances, when most animals appeared on TV, they were supposed to be the perfect little pets. No peeing, no pooping. All they had to do was jump through hoops of fire, or roll over and look cute. When I started doing television, I would give the puppies water. This would ensure a little pee here, a little puddle there. I *wanted* the audience to see that animals are real; they make mistakes like we do, they *get* embarrassed, they *are* embarrassing. So I think it was these moments, these things that have happened to me over the thousands of segments I've done on television, that established my reputation as this guy who just really loves animals. No bragging about how his dog can jump through hoops, or how his horse can take a bow, or how his goat can do this or his elephant or rhino do that. By letting people see that animals make mistakes, it made me real—and more important, it made the animals real.

On one particular episode of "Hour Magazine," the show was cohosted by Liberace. Poignantly, it was also Liberace's last TV appearance before he died.

Liberace owned a menagerie of twenty-six dogs. His favorites were several Chinese shar-peis. They're a wrinkly breed that looks like you dropped a piece of dough on the ground and stuck two eyes and a nose in it! Liberace had an amazing way with animals, relating to them as friends who just happened to have four legs, a tail, and a wet nose.

On this particular segment, we staged an animal fashion show. With typical Liberace panache, it was a glitter wedding for dogs, including a wedding gown that cost more than a thousand dollars, a groom's tuxedo, *and* best man and bridesmaids outfits. The band played a wedding march and the dogs "got married" on the show!

Interestingly enough, though I don't want to admit it now, I never quite understood the appeal of Liberace. And so I went out to do the show with kind of an attitude. Yet after meeting the man and working with him backstage and on-camera, I totally changed my opinion; he was fantastic. Liberace confided to me that he was thinking of buying a $60,000 doghouse. I advised him that having a mortgage on a doghouse might not be the best idea.

I believe Liberace's collection of pets was more than just an

Displaying the latest in winter-wear for pets on "Hour Magazine" with Gary Collins and guest Liberace.

extension of his grand style. This was a man faced with a constant pressure to maintain a larger-than-life image. The only completely nondemanding relationship he had was with his pets, and that's why he had so many. It's so ironic that, with him being such an animal lover himself, the last show Liberace ever did was with dogs.

Larry Takes the Stage

It was early fall 1978 when I received a call from the Northstage Theatre Restaurant, a major dinner theater in New York. They were casting the musical *Camelot*. The general manager of the theater, Lyn Perez, related that one of the performers they needed to cast for the production was a dog. Being the aficionado of great theater works, I asked what was *Camelot* all about, and what kind of dog would they need to fit the part? Lyn explained the dog named Horrid was the shaggy pet of King Arthur's court and belonged to a knight named Pellinore. In one scene, the Knight turns to the dog and King Arthur says, "What kind of dog is that?" and the Knight responds "It's a Pointer, sir." And the joke was, well, how could you tell which way he was pointing. Accordingly, we decided on an Old English sheepdog—assuming that because the rear end looked really similar to the front end, it would be perfect to tie in with the line. Lyn suggested buying an older dog, but I wanted to play my hunch—that a local shelter might have the perfect star.

Accordingly, I circled several shelters and pounds in search of a houndy, sheepy-looking dog that we could adopt, save a life, and put in the show at the same time. It was just the right thing to do. At one particular shelter on Long Island I came across a beautiful three- or four-year-old Old English sheepdog. I went in there, looked at the dog, and said to the people behind the counter, "Excuse me, I'd like to adopt that dog." I'll never forget the woman behind the counter saying to me, "You can't adopt that dog because his paperwork has already been processed and he's going to be euthanized in a few hours."

"Wait a second," I said. "I'm here now to take the dog, and you're telling me that because the paperwork has been filed, the dog is going to be killed even though I'm ready to give him a second life?"

"That's the way it is," she responded. "I can't get the paperwork back" and blah blah blah blah!!

At that point I became extremely pissed off. "Wait a minute!!" I shouted. "You're telling me . . . let me just understand this: I want the dog, the dog is still alive, but you're going to kill the dog because of the paperwork. OK, I'm going to the phone, and I am going to give my friends at *Newsday* a call and see how the press feels about this story." She ran back in the shelter and got a supervisor. Well, they tried to dicker about policy, but I left with the dog. It turned out that the dog had been picked up a couple of times by the pound and had belonged to a really irresponsible owner that couldn't have cared less about it. The dog also had a little bit of an aggressive tendency. In any case, I fell in love with the dog and took him back to the theater to introduce him to Lyn.

The training began, and everyone just adored the dog. Appropriately, the cast and crew bestowed a regal new name upon him: Sir Lawrence. The media department at the theater played up the whole ordeal as "From Wags to Riches"—and the press was charmed by it:

BROADWAY-BOUND HOUND PUTS
HIS BEST FOOT BACKWARD
(Page One, *New York Post*);

A DOG'S LIFE: FROM DEATH ROW TO CAMELOT
(*Newsday*).

Even numerous television shows followed this true-life canine version of *Pygmalion*.

Part of the training included Larry entering the stage one way and then exiting walking backwards. No major task you may think, but remember, this was dinner theater. It's difficult enough to get a dog to respond under normal circumstances, let alone when you have the aroma of prime rib wafting from the front row of the theater. Despite the temptations, the dog performed superbly. Everyone fell in love with Larry, and the show ran for almost eight months. I, too, was there every single night singing ". . . In short there's simply not, a more congenial spot, for happily ever aftering than here in Camelot!" Even in my sleep, God knows.

Inevitably, the long commute back and forth to the show became exhausting. One of the actors in the show who loved the dog volunteered to keep Larry at one of the apartments at the theater. I agreed, but I reserved the right to come and check on Larry regularly. One night when I visited the theater, I found cock-roaches swimming in and around Larry's water bowl. Well, that was enough. I slipped on his leash and that was Larry's final performance in the show. (The press picked up on that story as well.)

Larry lived with me to be a ripe old age of twelve and a half to thirteen years. He was truly a great dog, and we spent many hours playing together. He had this aggressive streak, so I taught him to take it out on me. I would say, "Larry, get me." In other words, he loved everyone else, but when I told him to "get me," he would let his aggressive behavior out and he would come over and jump on me in a playful way. As Larry got older, he had difficulty with steps, so I built a ramp in the backyard that helped him keep his dignity. He was a super-duper dog, and I miss him dearly.

Merv Griffin

I was in Los Angeles doing a spokesperson tour for the Pets Are Wonderful Council. This was an organization sponsored by the pet food industry to help promote good responsible pet ownership and from time to time I would act as their spokesperson. This simply meant I would go to various cities to talk about the goodness of owning pets, or why it was a positive experience to own a pet. In any case, I was in Los Angeles doing one of these spokesperson tours when I got a call from the producer of the Merv Griffin show. Now, Merv Griffin is *everyone's* idol. His show was *the* one to be on! They invited me to be a guest and asked me to do a segment on the world's biggest dogs. Well, how was I supposed to do this in Los

Angeles? Part of doing what I do for a living is finding different kinds of animals on the spur of the moment and then finding people willing to transport them to wherever they're needed. Nonetheless, with great difficulty I put together the segment. I remember specifically I had to get a Russian wolfhound, an Irish wolfhound, a mastiff, a Great Dane, a Scottish deerhound, two Saint Bernards, a Newfoundland, and a Great Pyrenees. They were the biggest dog breeds in the world—and I had two of each.

The other guests on the show that evening were Victor Borge and Mariette Hartley. Now, Victor Borge was a big dog lover, but he had recently been bitten by a dog on one of the islands where he lived. And so, understandably, he was a little hesitant in dealing with the dogs I had brought.

The show started, and since Victor Borge and Mariette Hartley were on before me, they were out there when my segment started. The idea was for me to bring the dogs out one breed at a time, and, hopefully, they would stay. At the end of the segment, all sixteen of these giant dogs—males and females—would have to be there with me. My only hope was that they would all get along with each other. It was a beautiful sight, and no one had any idea about the knots in my stomach. I was petrified that we would have a major dog fight on live television.

Well, I did manage to get all of the dogs peacefully out on stage together. Mariette Hartley and Victor Borge came over from the couch area. Everyone was having a good time, which was fine, and they were oblivious to my fears. They started clowning around with the dogs, and I'll never forget this: Victor Borge went down on his knees and one of the dogs started mounting him. It was quite a funny piece. To add to that, Mariette Hartley tripped over the dogs.

The segment must have lasted seven or eight minutes, considered a mini-series in live TV! The unplanned stunts were hilarious and all the dogs got along famously. Mariette Hartley and Victor Borge both enjoyed themselves, Merv laughed uproariously, and it worked out super for everyone. The producers even called me back to do the show several times after that.

"The Mickey Mouse Club"

A year or so after "Hour Magazine" completed its successful eight-year run, my close friend Steve Clements, who had "discovered" me for "Hour Magazine," informed me that, as his next production, he would be the executive producer for Disney's new "Mickey Mouse Club," which was going to be taping in Orlando, Florida, at Disney World. So Steve packed his bags and headed south. While he was spending a lot of time in Orlando, his wife, Judy, continued to live in Los Angeles. I was flying to L.A. at least once a month, and actually had dinner with his wife more than he did! I even called him one day saying, "Hey, Steve, your new stereo is really nice," knowing he hadn't been home since it arrived!

During the conversation, he asked me if I'd like to be the regular pet authority on the show. Having grown up with the "Mickey Mouse Club," I couldn't envision myself at forty years of age wearing the Mouse ears and saying "Why? Because we *like* you!" But how could I resist the nostalgia of it—I had been a big fan of Spin and Marty on the original "Mickey Mouse Club," and who didn't want to marry Annette Funicello? Or be like Cubby? It would be my little piece of television history. So, we brainstormed and they christened me the "Creature Keeper." I would have the opportunity to go to Disney World (which was a brand-new facility then, the official grand opening hadn't even taken place) twice a month for segments with different animals.

I would be taping the first show on Wednesday and I had tickets for a Tuesday flight. On Monday, New York suffered a major snowstorm, which meant delays at the airports. On top of that, a pilot's strike was in effect at one of the airlines, and there was some talk that pilots from other carriers were going to honor it. Well, there was no way I was going to miss that taping. So, at 9:00 P.M. Monday, I loaded up Tige, our cat Mowdy, and Fay (not necessarily in that order), got into my four-wheel-drive truck, and off we went—slowly. The snow and subsequent ice storm lasted all the way through Virginia. I figured that if we drove through the night, we'd get to Florida in time to relax in the late afternoon and get a really good night's sleep. Fat chance. Because of the storm, it took nine hours to travel the first three hundred miles. Then, somewhere around Savannah, Georgia, I got a toothache the likes of which I had never felt before. I was crazy with pain, but I decided to tough it out. Three quarters of the way through Georgia I realized that if I didn't have something done very quickly I was going to rip the tooth out myself. Mowdy and Tige weren't sure what my bizarre behavior was all about, but those two little angels knew something was wrong, so they sat ever so still, not even asking to go for a walk. Now we're in the middle of I-don't-know-where, Georgia. The next big city is Jacksonville, Florida. I'm screaming with pain. At ten o'clock Tuesday night—twenty-five hours after we started—we located a dentist willing to see some stranger off the street. Well, I got all shot up with Novocain and begged for a couple of prescriptions to help me through the next few days. Luckily we found a pharmacy that was open till midnight. Off we continued to Orlando, which, unbeknownst to me, was still three hours away. We finally rolled in at 3:00 A.M.—thirty hours after we left New York. We had to be at the taping at seven in the morning, so, after only three hours' sleep, we got up and went to the studio. How appropriate: It was "Anything Can Happen Day," and I did a studio spot with a stageful of dalmatians—sort of a takeoff on the original 101 dalmatians, with 70 to 80 on the set of the "Mickey Mouse Club." The segment came off incredibly well—the Disney people really liked it, and the new Mouseketeers were very bright and fun to work with. Even Mickey was happy.

Obviously, the "Mickey Mouse Club" of 1985 had matured considerably since the MMC of 1955. Following the usual fun pieces we did with the animals, the kids would slam dance rather than sing the "M-I-C—See you real soon—K-E-Y" song that I remembered from the "Mickey Mouse Club." It took a little getting used to, but it was a fascinating time for me.

Another of the demos I did on the show was amazing, really fun. The Creature Keeper brought on miniature animals: miniature goats and horses, *and* a miniature jackass. Visually, it was adorable to see the Mouseketeers surrounded by these pint-size animals. The kids were just fascinated by them, and the questions they asked were much more intelligent than some of the questions I get from adults. So it was one of the most enjoyable things I have ever done. Almost every appearance I made on the Club fell on "Anything Can Happen Day," and one episode I did had me bringing on my reptilian friends—an alligator, some very large venomous snakes, and sizable lizards. And then I did another segment on turtles and brought on maybe fifteen or twenty different types of turtles and tortoises. Again, the kids were fascinated and we would go into the audience and let the children touch them.

One of the most original segments, in terms of animals, that I did for the new "Mickey Mouse Club" involved hosting a location piece, which is unusual. It originated from Camp De Baun, in my hometown of Oceanside, which was owned by a friend of mine, Craig De Baun. With all these city kids circled around, we brought in some very unusual animals, like a binturong (or Asian civet). It was a fascinating remote.

One of my all-time favorite segments was called "Rodent Mania," where I tried to give a positive image to rodents—people just don't like them. I brought on guinea pigs, rats, mice, and all different types of animals that are in the rodent family, just to let people know the good points about them. I figured, what better place to pitch for mouse equality? I had done this on "Hour Magazine," "Regis & Kathie Lee," "Saturday Morning Live"—just about every show I have appeared on. For some reason, though, every time I pitched the idea to my segment producer at the "Mickey Mouse Club," it was kicked back to me, with a short: "I don't think it's a good idea." Finally, while having lunch with Steve one afternoon at a restaurant in Orlando, I put the question to him, "Steve, what's with this 'no rodent' studio spot?"

"Warren," he said, "these people really think they work for a mouse. To bring a real mouse or a real rodent on the air would be considered a sacrilege." And then I began to comprehend (or pretended to).

I didn't think any job would be more fun than *being* the Crea-

With 8,000-pound Shamu, the Killer Whale at Sea World in San Diego. Some killer! Even he responds to my Hugs & Kisses.

ture Keeper and working with these very talented kids. Like the time the producers wanted to arrange a location piece down by the Living Seas. My companion was Mouseketeer Lindsay, who was a really cute kid. We filmed the segment at EPCOT Center, which has the world's largest aquarium, and this was one of my first opportunities to spend some time in the water with dolphins. I was in the company of several dolphins who guided me around a fascinating array of animals, including sharks and manatees, the lovable sea cows. These dolphins were incredibly bright and responsive; it was a fascinating couple of days and I was very fortunate to have them. The real reward for me in doing this on-location piece was that I was hitting an audience of millions of kids; it gave me the opportunity to relay to them the importance of saving animals like dolphins, manatees, tortoises, sharks—*all* the animals that needed saving. The audience was still impressionable. Sometimes it's too late to change adults' minds, but it's never too late to get to the kids.

One of my all-time favorite segments on the "Mickey Mouse Club" was the bug demo. No one ever does a studio spot on bugs, so I decided that I was going to introduce Madagascar hissing cockroaches, bugs called walking sticks, all different varieties of roaches, dozens of various crickets, and praying mantises: "Bugs of the World." It was one of the first times this was ever shown on a television show—kids are really fascinated by bugs. At the time, my producer said to me, "Warren, you know kids could care less about bugs," but he was off-base. When I was a kid, bugs fascinated me and one of my prized possessions was an ant farm. So I fought for it, and I really felt like the "bug champion" when they all agreed it was a winner.

The "Mickey Mouse Club" gave me the opportunity to do things I had never done before. For example, as I've said before, I am basically a shy person. I would never choose to sing in public, but in this case it was not an elective: At the end of each show that I appeared in, I was required to come out with the Mouseketeers, dance around a little bit, and accompany them in singing the new Mickey Mouse Rap song. Talk about feeling sheepish! What fascinates me to this day, though, wherever I am in this country, kids (who are much older now!) will come up and say to me "Hey, you're the Creature Keeper from the 'Mickey Mouse Club.' You're the guy we used to watch on television." And every once in a while I still get a residual check. I guess the "Mickey Mouse Club" is going to live forever and is being shown somewhere in the world as we speak. It's one of those "rocking chair" memories; when I'm ninety-five years old I'm going to think back and say, "Hey, I was the Creature Keeper for the 'Mickey Mouse Club'!"

"Live! With Regis & Kathie Lee"

It's a mystery to me how my media career started. It was nothing I pursued or ever imagined doing—remember, I'm basically a shy person. However, as the years sail by, I realize how lucky I've been to have the opportunity to communicate with millions of people about my passion: their pets. How it started I don't know, and where it winds up is fate.

At one point I was concurrently the pet authority on "Hour Magazine" with Gary Collins, creating pet segments for "Saturday Morning Live" on Channel 5, and hosting "The Pet Show" on WOR Radio. At this time, there was a local talk show on ABC Television called "Good Morning New York," hosted by several different people, including Regis Philbin. The producer, Steve Ober, liked my pet segments on the other shows, so he asked me to appear on "Good Morning New York." I did a couple of segments that were hilarious and launched a very successful series of appearances.

Regis Philbin was then chosen as the regular host for "Good Morning New York," and he was joined by various female cohosts like Ann Abernathy and Cyndy Garvey; then, most entertainingly, with Kathie Lee Johnson (before becoming Mrs. Gifford). Buena Vista, the production company, decided to change the name to "Live! With Regis & Kathie Lee" and to syndicate the show nationally. Executive producer Michael Gelman asked me to come in one day for a segment on puppies. We called it "Puppy Mania." The piece was so successful that Buena Vista used it as their demo tape to sell the show nationally. "Live! With Regis & Kathie Lee" has now been on the air for eleven years and has enjoyed a tremendous amount of success. In my recurring role as the regular pet and animal authority, I have some *tails* to share.

One of the first pieces I did for the national show was a feature on rabbits. I brought fifteen different breeds on the show, one being a male Netherland dwarf, which weighed about two pounds and is the smallest kind of rabbit; another was the female Flemish giant, which is the largest, weighing in at about twenty pounds. I had all these rabbits running around the set, along with Regis and Kathie Lee down on their hands and knees. And yes, all of a sudden, the diminutive male Netherland dwarf jumped on top of Big Mama, the female Flemish giant, and hung on like Velcro. Because of the little guy's size they obviously couldn't mate, but it sure wasn't for a lack of trying—he went at it for about five minutes. The cameras were fixed on these two trying to breed, and it was absolutely hysterical. The *New York Post* even picked up the story!

As every "Regis & Kathie Lee" viewer knows, Michael Gelman is the executive producer for the show. Twelve years ago, Michael was just getting his start in the business as the producer of the "Regis Philbin Show" for the Lifetime cable network. He would call me to do a segment regularly and that's really where our friendship developed. Today, I watch in admiration as he tackles the pressure of producing a live hour of television five days a week and makes it look effortless. The success of the show does not rest solely on Regis and Kathie Lee's ability to entertain; credit is equally deserved by Michael Gelman for being so diverse. Who would think of putting Patti LaBelle and Warren with snakes on the same show—and make the whole thing work.

It's amazing how many people are involved in putting a show like this together. For example, I might get a call in the morning from segment producer Barbara Fight or Rosemary Kalikow, with whom I have worked over the years. The conversation might go like this: "Warren, we're going to be doing snakes next Wednesday, is that OK with you?" I would clear that and call all my snake contacts to get the snakes lined up for the show. Then the night before the show, maybe 9:30, they would call me up saying, "We're not doing snakes; we want to do something on rhinos or elephants or pigs." It's a very difficult show in terms of booking the animals, yet it has always worked out. We have always found the right animals to make each segment fun and interesting. There are many ways to do a segment on "Live! With Regis & Kathie Lee": the right way, the wrong way, Michael Gelman's way, Barbara Fight's way, and Rosemary Kalikow's way. During rehearsal, each one will tell me to do it a certain way—all different—and of course, I agree with them. Then, when it comes time for the segment, I do it my way. And when I finish, all three will say "See, I told you it would work!"

The show has given me the opportunity to work with all

Rob Lowe and wife adopting a stray pup I brought on "Live! With Regis & Kathie Lee." Talk about wags to riches!

different kinds of people. It has also given me the chance to teach so many about animals. If there's one thing I have gotten across on "Live!", it's educating the public about the concept of pets' emotions. Regis and Kathie—whom I adore by the way—are always (jokingly) criticizing me about my beliefs that animals really do have feelings, just like people. Thus, no matter what animal I bring on the show, and it really does vary, they all have emotions. I've had Madagascar hissing cockroaches, full-grown horses, llamas, bats, goats—you name it, we've had it on the show. And I have always tried to get across the message that they have feelings.

We also encourage the guests, or whichever celebrity is sitting in for either Regis or Kathie Lee when they vacation, to have some fun with the animals. I remember one segment we did called "Big Guys and Little Guys" when I brought on miniature horses and full-sized horses, also pygmy goats and full-sized goats. One of the guests on the show that day was Jackie Mason, and Gelman suggested, "Wouldn't it be funny if Jackie made his entrance on a horse?" I said, "Fine, we have a large horse out here and he's pretty mellow; we can put Jackie on him and I'll walk both of them in." Sure enough, Jackie Mason mounts the horse, and just before the stage doors opened up for Jackie's entrance, the horse took this incredible dump (sorry folks, there's no pretty way to say it) and paralyzed everyone in their tracks. It was really embarrassing! Jackie turned to me and said, "Thank God he did this now before I went on the show, because once I go on there, I'm really going to step in crap!"

One of the most famous segments I ever did was when Michael Gelman asked me to bring on some fleas and ticks. Well, where does one find live fleas and ticks? A breeder, of course (yes, they do exist). Much to Michael's amazement, I said "no problem" and showed up with the insects.

As I've said, the show is demanding because of time constraints. Sometimes I will have ten dogs lined up for a seven-minute segment on dogs of the world, but because "Host Chat" or the guest before me went a little long, my time is now down to three minutes to show ten dogs. God forbid I don't show them, because people have come from all over the tristate area to bring their dog in. Conversely, sometimes I get there and a guest didn't show or a segment ran short, and Michael will say, "OK, Warren, you have two and a half segments to do." It's called stretching, and thank God I always overbook—as opposed to underbook—so I have more than we need.

One of my favorite show memories was when Tony Danza was a fill-in host. Regis was present, and Kathie Lee was out. Generally speaking, when Kathie Lee is gone, women take her place; and when Regis is gone, men take his place. However, on this occasion, the show consisted of Tony Danza, Regis, and me. The segment I was doing was on pet massage. I brought three dogs on stage to be massaged: a Labrador retriever that I was going to demonstrate on, an Irish wolfhound for Regis to work, and a dachshund for Tony. So there we were, three macho guys sitting on the floor massaging dogs. Every time Regis went to massage his dog, Neil, the Irish wolfhound, would get up and walk around. However, when Tony or I massaged Neil, he was great. There was something about

Regis's technique that the dog didn't like. Another terrific fill-in host was Bill Cosby, who not only got down on his hands and knees to crawl along with a desert tortoise I brought on, but bobbed his head in and out ever so *slooowwwwly* to imitate him!

The staff on the show is very collaborative, and their brainstorming sessions involve everyone from the sound technicians and stage managers to the producers, director, and Regis and Kathie Lee, which is why they never run out of wacky ideas! Like the day

Michael Gelman giving me some last-minute tips before "Mr. Warren's Neighborhood."

segment producer Barbara Fight called with her typical rapid-fire sales pitch: "Warr, you're gonna love this one. We just got out of a show meeting and you're going to do your next segment not as Warren but as your sister Julie." Where is it in my contract that I'm a *cross-dressing* pet and animal authority? But on I went—I mean my *sister* Julie Eckstein went on with the animals. She wasn't exactly a sex symbol, but she definitely gave Mrs. Doubtfire a run for her money! At least I didn't have to sing—that time. A couple of years later, after another infamous staff idea session, Barbara once again breathlessly launched into the hard sell: "This is the best, Warr. We've decided to dress you up in a cardigan and dye your hair gray while you sit at a piano and sing 'It's a Beautiful Day in the Neighborhood' for Regis and Kathie and all the animals you bring to 'Mr. Warren's Neighborhood.'" Now, there are two things you will never see me do: dancing and/or singing. I'd rather be torn to bits by a twenty-foot great white, limb by limb. Nevertheless, they coax me into the most amazing situations, and I ended up crooning the tune—more like half howling—"Won't *you* be my *neighbor?*"

And talk about gratitude, after all that humiliation, can you believe the cast actually blames *my* appearances for three couches they've had to replace due to leaky pets!

The show has served as a major boost to my career. It's been an incredible journey; hard and trying at times, yet exhilarating. When my wife, Fay, passed away in 1990, they were unbelievably supportive. From Bobby the prop master to Regis and Kathie Lee themselves, they were there for me and said they would do whatever they could do to help. Thereby, over the years we have grown to be more than close friends. I have worked with people longer than I have with their staff, but as far as I'm concerned, "Live! With Regis & Kathie Lee" is a genuine family.

OTHER CAREER
MOVES

Spokesperson

It was in the early eighties that I first heard the term *spokesperson*, having no idea what a spokesperson was or what a spokesperson did. By way of personal experience, I came to find out that a spokesperson is someone who is paid to go on media, both print and electronic (television and radio), as well as participate in lectures and seminars for the purpose of promoting a specific product or theme. Many of the spokesperson tours I have been involved with were for nonprofit organizations. Others were spearheaded by the business sector, to develop or enhance a company or product to a targeted audience. Generally they were sparked by a public relations firm.

It was a fascinating thing to do and yet one of the most difficult jobs in the world. Years ago, I'd get $500 a day, plus $250 per diem for traveling, and boy, I thought I was being paid a fortune! One of the first spokesperson tours I did was on behalf of an organization called the Pets Are Wonderful Council. It was the idea of a p.r. firm in Chicago, bankrolled by the pet food industry. Their job was to hire spokespeople and book them around the country.

So they contacted me, as well as a couple of other people in the field of animal behavior—always with a celebrity overtone to it. At one point it was Betty White, succeeded by Rue McClanahan. Then it followed to Alan Thicke, then (I think) to Bill Cosby. In essence, PAWs (Pets Are Wonderful) would hire someone like myself to go to various cities to do all of the media; in this case talking about the importance of owning a pet as well as responsible pet ownership. Generally, the concept of the pet food industry was if you can talk about positive pet ownership then more people will have pets and more pet food would ultimately be sold.

What made the spokesperson role so challenging was the scheduling. There is no "down time." I was literally running after planes, going from city to city. It was not unusual to be in two cities in just one day. I might start early in the morning, doing the early morning radio shows in one city, then finish the day on the late evening radio shows in another. In between, it was a hectic dash—appearing around the clock on every television news program: the morning news, the noon news, the afternoon news, the five o'clock news, while squeezing in a trip to the local newspaper for some print ads and some photographs to be taken, all the while remaining alert for the all-important photo opportunity. It was important to appear "fresh" for each interview, as well as to remain focused on ways to work in the message of the tour's sponsor. I would literally arrive home after one of these tours hoarse and in a catatonic state.

This was my first step into spokesperson tours. After I had completed this tour, the public relations firm retained me for two or three years in a row to go to Los Angeles, Chicago, and wherever else. Following that, I was signed by the Ralston Purina Company to deliver the message for their program, Pets for People. Their plan was to have spokespeople travel around the country talking about the importance of pets for senior citizens. The concept was that the older dogs and the older cats that were more difficult to adopt would be the ideal match for seniors. Additionally, owning a pet would make seniors feel better, providing such health benefits as lowering blood pressure and alleviating stress. Pets give seniors a feeling of nurturing and help make them feel overall better about themselves. So this was the concept: To further encourage the adoptions, for anyone over sixty, Ralston Purina absorbed all the expenses associated with acquiring a pet—including veterinary visits, adoption fees, spaying or neutering services, collars, leashes, meal bowls, and a supply of Purina Dog Chow or Cat Chow.

I thought it was a great idea, so I went on tour in the company of the p.r. firm that worked for Ralston Purina. What I observed in my escorted tours was that this was not a high priority at the public relations firm. They assigned relatively young, recent school graduates (obviously without much experience) to tour with me. For the most part they all looked the same: they had to be youthful, they had to be attractive, and, above all, they had to be "perky." *Beyond* perky would be the description I would use.

Their mission was to make sure I'd arrive at the designated place on time, and (by hovering) to serve as a visual cue to "get the plug in" for the sponsoring company. This is when I grasped the term *plug*. Being an auto mechanic's son, a "plug" to *me* was something you put inside a car to stop the oil from leaking! But I found out that in the world of promotion, a plug was kind of like a commercial insert in the middle of the conversation, dropping in a name or an idea. For example, if I was talking about the Pets for People program and how good it was for seniors, I would say something like: "What a nice thing for Ralston Purina to be putting up the money for this."

I had completed several tours for Ralston Purina's Pets for People when they started a program called Pet Pal to raise awareness on kids and pets. I did a stint for that tour as well. It was fascinating because I met a lot of legendary people: the big celebrities in all the small towns around the U.S.A., the "super talents" of radio show hosts in St. Louis, Chicago, Boston, Nashville, and Memphis. Again it was a blur of endless cities, concentrated in very few days—simultaneously, I was running the kennel with Fay, trying to schedule media appearances around the country, writing a book, and still training animals. The hours and the time spent away were just absolutely incredible.

Because of the enormous time tours required, I had to become very selective about which ones I signed to do. One unusual cause that appealed to me came from a public relations company in New York that was representing United Action for Animals, a nonprofit organization seeking to eliminate animal research and testing. They were extremely well documented with regard to the abuse going on at some of the major universities in their experimentation on animals. The source of their documentation? Reports from biomedical journals and individual government reports. More than $4 billion of taxpayer money was being spent each year in this country on animal research and testing, much of it inhumane. United Action for Animals wanted to call attention to some of these problems that they felt needed a voice, so I was recruited to go on tour to the different cities and talk about the fact that animal experimentation for the most part was wrong, and even worse, 60 to 75 percent of this research was duplicative, killing millions of animals every year for no-goal experimentation.

In going out on this tour, I was hitting smaller cities—Lexington and Louisville, Kentucky; Virginia Beach, Virginia; Nashville and Memphis, Tennessee—with stops in various towns within those areas. The agenda was very difficult because at every stop I would be talking about the concept of universities' redundancy. And there was always some professor, veterinarian, or doctor at the studio to debate me on it. Luckily, it's been my field for many years, so it was not a difficult task to either win the debate or at least to come off in a tie. Everywhere I went, I was put in the hot seat and this was *before* Morton Downey, Jr. I remember one time we were talking with a veterinarian in, I believe it was Memphis, Tennessee. And because he was steadfast in the concept of how important medical experimentation was, it seemed as if he was accustomed to debating with the type of animal rights people who would stand up, yell and scream, and throw blood on people who wore fur. However radical my thoughts were, I was very well versed in what I was doing and I also knew that radical actions don't always get you the best results. Sometimes you have to kind of step back a little bit and say "What's going to get the point across the right way?"

Anyway, we were debating and he started to spout on about "how all you animal rights people are the same" and in my reply to him (and this is probably the greatest line I've ever used), I said, "You know what, I'm sitting here, I'm not an abolitionist. What I am against is the redundancy and the ludicrous experimentation going on."

"Like what?" he asked.

"Well, you know, a hundred thousand dollars was given to a university in the northeast to study the effects of a certain type of drug on *horses*. Then a university down South got the same amount of money to do the same study on *ponies*. Physiologically, they are exactly the same—the redundancy factor. One university received X amount of money to study the effects of certain drugs and chemicals on black rats, another university was granted a similar amount to conduct a study on *white* rats, and it just goes on and on—redundancy."

He countered with, "Well, it has to be done, how else would anyone know?"

"Well, if you have to do certain experimentation," I said, "how about a national clearinghouse where, if university A wants to find out the results of a certain test before they kill, maim, or mutilate animals, they see if it's been done already and can use those results." Plus, with the advent of modern technology, computerized cells and tissue samples were enabling researchers to come up with the same results, therefore dispensing with the need to do live animal research. Along with many others, I maintained that many of these live animal studies were done more for money than results. But it was such a controversial issue and so hotly challenged, that it was probably the most strenuous tour I ever did.

I also signed on for a tour sponsored by Tyco Toys. Now, you are probably sitting there and reading this and saying, "OK, Tyco Toys, Warren?" Their public relations firm approached me in 1991 asking me what I thought of a product that Tyco was coming out with. They were stuffed animals: a Plush Puppy and Kitten Caboodle that were kind of lifelike and made puppy and kitten noises. The concept was: Wouldn't these be a good idea for teaching kids how to handle puppies and kittens prior to getting one? Sometimes kids can be really rough by pulling tails and ears and hitting and biting and whatever kids do to pets. So I felt it was a good idea and I went down and met with some of the bigwigs of Tyco Toys in southern New Jersey.

For the first time in all the years that I'd been doing tours, I never realized that as a spokesperson you should be requesting first class airfare, staying in Mobil Guide hotels rather than Motel Six, and getting reimbursed for certain out-of-pocket expenses. I'd be flying Big Apple Air while my television cohorts were flying first class on planes with no propellers—imagine that! It just never occurred to me to ask for those things, and (surprise!) no one who could *afford* to be forthcoming *was*. But the Tyco Tour marked the first time I had Howard West, my manager, negotiate the deal with the public relations firm, and it was kind of rewarding. Yes, I did fly first class everywhere; yes, I did stay at class hotels everywhere; yes, I got paid more money per day than I had ever been paid before. But in return, they extracted their pound of flesh: I traversed the country doing television shows from five in the morning until midnight. I was never so tired in my life.

I traveled with the requisite public relations young woman. Remember: attractive, bubbly and Up With People. She was all those things as we crisscrossed the South from Atlanta, Georgia, to Dallas, Texas; Fort Worth; Houston—just all over the place. It was a warm and fuzzy tour, and thinking back on it, I could have demanded whatever I wanted because the concept was promising, and who else would have been good enough to tie in realistic animal behavior with a toy? You know, sometimes, ego aside, I am that good.

In the years before 1984, prior to all these spokesperson tours, I would go into clients' homes and see the husbands traveling, and I would say to myself, "God, I'd *love* to see parts of the country I've never seen before." Let me tell you, folks, be careful what you wish for. Still, these spokesperson tours were an incredible education for me, and a prelude for what was to come, having not yet written any books. My mother maintains that "People are the same everywhere," but traveling was really an education. I made contacts and friends at media places all around the country, so when I went on book tours, it was like visiting old friends. As lucrative as the spokesperson role can be, though, I'm fairly limited by my personal code: Any product I endorse has to be one that I would use on my own pets, or a position that I have held close to me. *If you don't have your word, what do you have?*

Another aspect of being a spokesperson for which I've been approached but won't participate in is called the "damage control" expert. If your product or service has been compromised, I'm not the one to call about repairing or rehabilitating its image. I'm really unforgiving when it comes to protecting our animals because *we are the only voice they have.*

A Boy and His Dog

It always amazes me: You never know what the next call coming into our office will bring. It could be someone wanting their dog trained, it could be a media appearance; it was fairly unpredictable and *always* interesting! Like that spring day in 1981 when we were contacted by a woman who worked for a large public relations firm—I believe it was called Peter Martin Public Relations.

This firm was in charge of a massive publicity campaign by the Buster Brown Company to be based on the good-hearted but mischievous boy and his loyal pup. She filled me in on the history of the two: Buster Brown and Tige (short for Tiger) were an overnight sensation when they appeared as the nation's first full-page color comic strip in 1902. Two years later they were sold to a company that has made children's clothes in their names ever since.

They seemed real because they were based on the actual

family of cartoonist Richard Outcault. The boy and his dog were kept famous by radio announcer "Smiling Ed" McConnel in the 1940s but lost "market share" when they turned to TV advertising after World War II.

The p.r. company's vision now was to reintroduce Buster and Tige to a new generation of youngsters via this campaign, which would include a cross-country tour as well as other parts of the world.

They had bought an American Staffordshire terrier puppy from a breeder, and they had hired a trainer whose technique just wasn't working out. Deftly, she stated, "We don't like his work, Warren. Would you consider working with the dog... ultimately training him for the Buster Brown Corporation?" I replied, "Well, first I have to meet the dog and find out what's involved, what kind of training it would entail."

So I drove into Manhattan to this really impressive public relations office; it just struck me what a really classy office it was, I mean thousands of dollars in antiques in the office and so many people working there, scurrying around.

Anyway, I spotted the dog in a kennel, and his eyes just said to me, "Wow, this isn't a dog; this is a man in a little dog's suit," and that was my introduction to Tige, whose real name by the way was Cochise. He, of course, had the huge mastiff head and his "suit" was tan and white.

I could see that whoever had been working with Cochise was not really a loving trainer, because this was the type of dog that you were going to get a lot more out of with a hug and a kiss than you would with any kind of training collar. So I spent a few minutes with the dog and sat down with the owners of the p.r. company, accompanied by Elizabeth Daggert, who was the representative from the Buster Brown Corporation (which was located in Chattanooga, Tennessee). By the end of this "power meeting," I decided that I would take it on. It sounded like an exciting thing, as I explained to Fay. Yes, we would be doing a lot of traveling, and if I couldn't go with the dog I would send one of my trainers. But it seemed like a lot of fun, with not a major amount of training called for.

I grasped the most important concept: that Tige was a great-

My dog Tige. We didn't live in a shoe, but after Fay died, he truly got me through the toughest time in my life.

looking dog who had to be smothered by children everywhere he went. Whether he was doing a store appearance or a National Safety Council commercial, he always had to be around people and kids and react properly, which was kind of an interesting task because kids just marveled at Tige. He had his own clothing, his own outfits to wear.

Anyway, it started like this: When I took Tige, the arrangement was that they were going to be paying me a monthly fee that included training and care of the dog, and they would be taking care of expenses when we traveled with the dog. The day I picked up the dog, as I was leaving, they casually asked me, "Oh, by the way, you will be ready by next Wednesday?" I looked at them and said, "Ready by next Wednesday for what?" They had planned an industry show at a major New York City showroom for the buyers of children's clothing. It was to be the first roll-out of the upcoming campaign, so it was incredibly important to them. They had hired an actor to dress up as Buster Brown who would be on stage with Tige. From off stage, I would have to command Tige to jump onto a chair, face the audience, turn around, and bark at certain commands—all while he was dressed in his Tige jacket, by the way.

Now I'm *good*, but having only three *days* to do this was more than a little pressure! Still, we did the performances at the show and Tige responded just beautifully. As time went on, we spent a lot of time training for the dozens of appearances he made. Then they decided that Tige would do some work in Puerto Rico, but to save a little money, Tige would fly there with Elizabeth, the lady who represented the Buster Brown Corporation. And I remember being really disturbed when they got on a plane, because basically it takes me a half hour (not even) to fall in love with a dog, and I was in love with Tige. Yet the company owned the dog, so I couldn't force them to take me or one of my trainers. And off they went.

In the middle of the night I got this frantic phone call: Tige had this woman in her motel room and he was chewing on her feet! He would keep charging her whenever she tried to get out of the room, and she was petrified. I mean, Tige was a powerful dog— he was one of those breeds classified as a pit bull. He had an exceptionally powerful body, with a big head and a heart of gold. Anyway, she kept pleading, "What can I do, I can't get out of the motel room. The dog's charging me, he's attacking me!" I told her to simply pick up the leash and just be a bit more assertive. The next day I had to dispatch one of my staff to Puerto Rico so the show could continue with Tige there. See, they wanted to save a few bucks, but you have to have the pros with you! Anyway, they made it back and I resumed touring around the country with Tige—throughout the Midwest, across New England, and down South.

One day we were in Kissimmee, Florida, at a place called Circus World. We were going to be in a big circus parade, with Tige and an actor playing Buster Brown being pulled by an elephant, similar to the old Disney Main Street parades. For no apparent reason, Tige was unresponsive—as good a dog as he was, he just didn't like being around these elephants, especially looking at the back side of one—and I can't blame him, it's not a pretty sight. He became a little rambunctious that day and it took me a good couple of hours of exposure and socializing, working with him and the elephants, to get the response I needed. It was critical because the cameras were shooting a special, Tige's Circus World, as well.

We wound up back in New York City at, believe it or not, the Buster Brown Museum. Yes, they actually had a palace of memorabilia that includes Buster Brown shoes from the old "Andy's Gang," Andy Devine. Then the company decided the campaign was over and Tige was going to be retired. "What do you mean, retired?" I said. This dog had been with me for more than two years at this point, and I was absolutely in love—this was *my* dog! They replied, "The dog will have to go back to the breeder. We have a legal contract and that's just the way it is." Totally distraught, I told Fay, "They can take the dog back, I'll let them do that; but then I'm going to kidnap this dog. No one is going to take Tige away from me!"

Anyway, he went back to the breeder, who was going to be using Tige as a stud dog. Maybe if Tige could have made a choice he would have said, "Warren, what are you doing? I'm going to be a stud dog for the rest of my life—leave me alone!" We found out where he was, and I doggedly pursued the veterinarian/breeder of the American Staffordshire Breeding Kennel outside Philadelphia. "Listen," I said to him, "here's the scenario: You have a lot of dogs there. Tige has been with me for two years and you know he'll have the most incredible care possible. What do I have to do to get him?" The breeder was reluctant to part with him, but strictly because Tige, being the Buster Brown dog, was a "hot" stud and commanded a higher fee than his other Am. Staffs. But everyone has their price and he relented, "For $500, he's yours."

I said, "What time are you open till?"

"I'll be here until nine tonight," he replied. I packed Fay in the car and off we went. Believe me, it was touch and go getting the $500 to pay for Tige—coincidentally, it was also our wedding anniversary.

We drove back to the kennel, but they brought up the wrong dog! "Wait a second, that's not Tige!" I cried.

"Oh, yes it is," they insisted.

"Come on now, I know Tige" . . . who came up just jumping all over me, hopped in the car, and never left me again. Tige and Fay and I were so incredibly bonded; there was no closer relationship.

The final payoff is that because of Tige I became established in the theatrical field. After the Buster Brown days, a lot of people were calling me—would I train this dog for an MTV shoot, or a magazine layout, or a VH-1 filming?

The Kennel Years

I have always been a dreamer, and one of my biggest dreams was owning a kennel. I wanted to create a place where I could board dogs and cats so that when people went away on vacation, they would feel secure knowing their pets were in good hands. At that time there was nothing in the New York area that I could recommend to my clients, so I told Fay I wanted to open up a kennel. She was not really enthusiastic about this, because we were both quite busy, but I thought it was time to make the move.

I started scouting locations and I found a place in my own town of Oceanside, in an oil complex that was surrounded by oil tankers. If there was ever a fire, we would all be blown to smithereens. However, it was one of the only spots I could find that was zoned for a kennel. It looked like a big Quonset hut, very gloomy and depressing, but with a fresh coat of paint, I rhapsodized about the possibilities. I purchased fifty gallons of paint and did the entire building in a sunshine yellow. You could even see it when you flew into Kennedy Airport because of its bright color!

We opened the building, all twelve thousand square feet of it, yet we had not come up with a name. We tossed a couple around, and I came up with Pet Resorts International. It was for pets, it was a resort, and we had clients from all over the world who would leave their animals with us. Pet Resorts International could accommodate up to 110 different pets at one time. Shortly after the opening, we received a letter from the attorneys at Merv Griffin Productions in Atlantic City. It had kind of slipped my mind that Merv Griffin had a place in Atlantic City called Resorts International. Hence, they were writing to say we could not use the name Pet Resorts International because it was too close to their name. I remember arguing with them, saying that we didn't have slot machines for the schnauzers. It was simply a boarding facility. I politely told them they could sue me, but nothing ever surfaced. They left us alone and Pet Resorts International proudly opened its doors.

We were quite successful for the first six months. We had more than one hundred dogs and cats, and were pretty much booked solid. The biggest challenge we ran into early on was finding the right staff—and we needed about twelve people.

The runs at the kennel were very large. Most kennels have an indoor/outdoor run situation. Our kennels individually were six feet wide by ten feet long, which is a *very* large area for a dog to be in. We did it this way because some people wanted two dogs kept together. But we also felt that by giving a dog more space, it wouldn't feel confined. These were dogs that were accustomed to running around a split level or a Park Avenue duplex, so keeping them in a small area was just not the right thing to do. Besides being enormous, these kennels were not what you would normally see at a boarding facility. Ours were portable—not sunk in the ground—and we chose them so that we could lift them up, move them, and really get to the areas we needed to clean. We spent an astronomical amount on chemicals alone—by the truckload—for odor control, bacteria control, everything possible just to make sure that the kennel always smelled good, looked good, and was safe for the animals.

We had to move these kennels every day, and they were extremely heavy, so I had to come up with a system. I went to my toolbox and built what looked like two giant skateboards that each kennel would slide onto. We could then transport each kennel from one area to another.

Prior to opening Pet Resorts, there were a lot of innovations I wanted to offer. Besides the physiological basic ABCs for the animals—getting them all their shots, making sure they were all in good health and didn't come down with any diseases—we knew we had to deal with the psychological stress and anxiety the animals would suffer being away from mom and dad. It was a major challenge for any kennel owner. And this was something I had to confront. "OK," I said, "how are we going to make these pets happy? How are we going to keep their minds mentally stimulated?"

There were several things we did; one may sound a little crazy to most people. We actually had the owners send postcards or call us from where they were, not only to check up on their dogs but to see if their dogs, in fact, wanted to talk to them on the phone. We brought the dog or cat to the phone and had the owner talk to it, if they wanted to do it that way. Or if they sent a card to their pet, a staffer would sit down with the cat or dog and read to the animals, which would make them feel better because they were getting a lot of attention.

I also decided to put in a Jacuzzi. I know what you're thinking. But if we had an older dog or a dog with an arthritic problem, we would use some warm water and swirl the Jacuzzi. It made the dog feel better. The animals absolutely adored it.

Because of the unpredictability of the weather in New York, we had separate indoor and outdoor exercise areas. The indoor area was like a large hallway that was 15 feet wide and maybe 150 feet long with little sandboxes for them to play in, obstacle courses to work with, and balls, Frisbees, and a full toy box. We had a similar setup outdoors. Also, for the dogs who really wanted some mental stimulation and work, there was an entire obstacle course on the side of the kennel that included barrel jumps, hoop jumps, tunnels, and all different activities they could do. And we had a small swimming pool, where we would pick the dogs up, slip on the doggy life preserver, and hand them over for a swim with a staff member.

When you entered the kennel for the first time your immediate impression was of a nursery school, because we encouraged people to bring items from home. So, many a dog arrived with its "blankey," or a cat was brought in accompanied by a stuffed animal. One day a large van pulled up with two rottweilers who were being left at the kennel. The owner said, "We haven't left our dogs here before, but you came really highly recommended, and we know our friends bring things from home. One of our rotties is older and she just loves to hang out in a reclining chair. Do you mind if we bring this recliner into the kennel and put it where the dogs are going to be kept?" Luckily, our six-by-ten kennels could accommodate the Lazy Boy. I'll never forget the sight of this beautiful rottweiler, Gretchen, sprawled out on her recliner!

There was music in the background and TVs every few kennel spaces so the dogs could watch if they wanted to. And we took requests. I would ask each owner, "What type of music or what type of TV program does your dog or cat like?" And we would try to accommodate accordingly.

If an owner brought in a pet who was overweight, we'd put it on a little reducing diet and increase its activity level with some pet aerobics, which was about the time that our book by the same name was released. We considered the mental attitude of the dog as being very important, and I believe we were the first kennel to really take that into consideration. Obviously, the kennel was way ahead of its time in terms of what we were offering. It's interesting now that, so many years later, more and more kennels are following our lead and it's a good thing.

Not content with just making the surroundings ideal, we

promised to feed each pet whatever it was fed at home. And since we boarded more than a hundred animals, we needed dozens of different kinds of cat and dog food; we were continually stocking and restocking more than thirty commercial lines. Tons and tons of food were constantly being delivered because we required so much variety.

The kennel developed an incredible reputation, and its appeal extended far beyond Long Island. Not only were we the dog and animal trainers to the stars, but Pet Resorts International was now the kennel of the stars. Word spread quickly to the Upper East Side and the Upper West Side of Manhattan that we were open, and we were just inundated with celebrities—not just recognizable names but financial wizards, famous producers and directors, presidents of Fortune 500 companies. It was fascinating to see a Rolls-Royce or a stretch limo Cadillac pull up in front of the kennel with the chauffeur getting out and opening the back door for a schnauzer or a cockapoo.

One of the anxieties I had at the kennel was "petnapping," which may sound a little eccentric to some people—why would anyone steal a dog or cat? Well, let me give you an example. At one time in the kennel we hosted Cheryl Tiegs's and Tony Peck's dog Martini; Lily Tomlin's associate's dog, Diva; David Letterman's two dogs, Bob and Stan; Princess Yasmin Khan's dog; Mrs. Woolworth's—yes, *the* Mrs. Woolworth's—dog; a New York senator's dog; the dog of a Long Island congressman; and while she was running for the vice-presidency, Geraldine Ferraro had her Sammy there.

So what was my fear? I was incredibly apprehensive that someone would come in and take these pets hostage, looking for some type of financial gain in return. Obviously, we staffed the kennel twenty-four hours a day, but the labor pool from which we hired kennel workers tended to be transient. They'd work at one kennel for a year or two and then move on to a different place, one after another. It's not the type of career you choose to take on for the rest of your life.

So basically I was always sleeping with one ear and one eye open, making sure everything was safe. I remember popping up many times in the middle of the night saying, "Fay, I'm just going to get in the car and take a ride over to the kennel to check things out and make sure things are going OK."

In addition, it wasn't the kind of business that if someone didn't show up it was OK. We had dogs and cats that were on insulin or needed specific medications, and we had to make sure those animals were taken care of. We also had to anticipate other conflicts that would arise. This was New York, after all. What if the heat stopped working in the dead of winter, or the cooling system crashed in August? What was going to happen to all these animals?

And because we were located down by the water, we also had problems with dampness, even though we had these incredibly large heaters. It was incredible the amount of money I went through, $1,500 to $2,000 a month, just in oil bills alone! Yet the floors always seemed a little damp. Finally I said to Fay, "We've got to figure out a way to do this." I had read in a country magazine about wood-burning stoves that could be converted from fifty-five gallon drums that were very safe. "You know, if we burn wood, it will have a very drying effect on the floor if we put them in strategic areas," I suggested to her. So we bought two kits, picked up the fifty-five gallon drums and made the wood-burning stoves. Then I started buying wood by the truckload, taking my new chain saw whenever I had an hour or two and cutting the wood up myself.

In the summer, because we were right on the water, we always had a nice, cool breeze coming in. But the kennel itself, at twelve hundred square feet, was just too large to air-condition. On really

Diva, Lily Tomlin's assistant's Dobi, boarding with me in New York. First time I was exposed to purple hair—on the owner, not the dog.

hot days, the fans were on and we even put hoses on the roof just to make it even cooler in the kennel, which the dogs absolutely adored.

My favorite reminiscence of the kennel years is that when the dogs went home, always healthy and happy, each one received a report card signed by me. Every kennel had a chart on it, telling me how the dog was eating and a description of its personality—did it seem depressed, was it a little anxious, was it showing any aggressive behavior? Was it drinking water? What was its stool like? What was its urine like? Were its eyes looking bright? Did its coat look bright? Fay or I checked these on a daily basis, and if we noticed any problem, we would take care of it right away. And it seemed worth the entire effort when we saw the happy faces of the people and their pets as they were reunited.

But Fay and I were consumed by the workload, running over 125 hours a week. We added a retail boutique at the kennel selling dog food and pet accessories. We had fourteen trainers on the road and, now, twenty staff members at the kennel, including two full-time secretaries. I was a regular employer at this point in my life. I even had to go down to New York City to be assigned Workmen's Compensation. The state felt working with dogs was more dangerous than being a fireman, and no one would insure me other than the state insurance fund. The fee for this was astronomical.

In order to head off any potential problems, I had to wear a beeper at all times. It would beep if the temperature in the kennel dropped below a certain temperature, if there was smoke in the kennel, or any other crisis. My home phone would ring in the middle of the night and we would dart to the kennel to assess the problem. It was a twenty-four-hour, seven-day-a-week job, and was really the most incredible undertaking on my part.

If a kennel worker called in sick, then I was there at three o'clock in the morning giving a cat its insulin shot, or Fay was there at 10:00 P.M. grooming dogs and bathing cats. The kennel would not have been so demanding had I not also had the training school, started doing the media, writing the books, traveling, and doing all the things that I was involved in at the same time. I admit, however, that I am just one of those people who looks for immediate gratification and I often take something on before I'm actually ready to do it. We were nearly collapsing from the pressure of our extremely busy schedule, but Fay and I were dedicated to keeping the kennel running in an efficient and effective manner ... *and* I was busy launching my *next* venture!

I decided to make Pet Resorts International *more* than just a boarding place for one's pets. My brainstorm? "Maybe I'll start giving demonstrations!" So I started handling police dogs and applied for a federal and New York State license for narcotics at the kennel so I could work with police departments who dealt with narcotics. It's very difficult to obtain a narcotics license, and they sent an inspector down who did a background check. I passed and was finally granted a federal drug license to buy drugs. Now I needed some marijuana so I could teach dogs to sniff it out. Unfortunately, purchasing marijuana legally was not an easy task. The closest place to me was the National Institutes of Health in Bethesda, Maryland. I jokingly said to the inspector that it was easier to buy pot on the streets of New York than to buy it legally. (He didn't laugh.)

We started giving demonstrations and, by publicizing them, we drew a lot of visitors to the kennel. We had one particular event that drew a large crowd. It was on attack dogs, police dogs, and antikidnap dogs. We had advertised the demonstration in the local paper and generated a crowd of over 150 people. Even my parents were in the audience. Part of the demonstration had me playing the role of the criminal and the dogs would have to attack me. That was no big deal—I'd been doing that for years. However, unbeknownst to the crowd, and due to the anxiety of the situation, I became really nervous. And during one of the attacks, I fell and one of the dogs got me in the chest. When I say got me in the chest, I mean his teeth ripped the skin and it took about twenty-five to thirty stitches to sew me back up. No one knew I was bitten until I took a break and walked into the kennel. Fay came in and saw that my shirt was drenched in blood, as did my mom, who, in turn, panicked. Well, I put some tape on the wound, finished the demonstration and then went over to the hospital to get stitched up. Afterward, Fay told me quite strongly that demonstrations were no longer going to be part of the kennel.

Although the kennel years were very gratifying, it was a time I look back on with some guilt because it was extremely arduous. We were a married couple who hardly ever got to see each other, and "quality time" for us meant comparing blisters and bad backs. More of the stress was on Fay, because she was running the business. I was out on the road early in the morning doing the training, not to mention keeping up with all my media appearances. So I had maybe an hour a day to shoot into the kennel. The time was just too stressful.

Despite these challenges, we kept the kennel for almost five years. During this time Fay was diagnosed with diabetes, and everything was really taking a toll on both of our lives. After some soul-searching and with tears filling my eyes, I decided that it was no longer worth it. As much money as the kennel was making (it was grossing quite a bit each year) and as much fun as running it was, now was the time to move on. But first we had a dilemma: We had eight stray dogs, six chickens, six ducks, twenty-two rabbits, and two pigs. Now, I lived on Long Island, which was pretty much a suburban area. If I closed the kennel, I couldn't keep them at home. What was I going to do with all my animals? We had to find a place for them.

Upstate New York

I have always loved upstate New York. And another of my dreams has been to own a farm in the area, a cross between Mr. Greenjeans and Oliver in "Green Acres." We started looking about an hour outside New York City. What the realtors were showing us for what we could afford was basically a lean-to: two posts with a piece of canvas over it. The other properties on the "caravan of homes" were of the "fixer-upper" type, which was a piece of ground with a board lying on it. Consequently, we were advised that if we wanted to buy affordable property in upstate New York that was livable, we would have to venture farther up, farther up, and farther up. When we were just about to run out of map, we came across the delightful little town of Cobleskill, New York, located in the northern region of the Catskills in the county of

Schoharie. That's about one half hour west of Albany, and one half hour east of Cooperstown.

Many Europeans settled in this neck of the woods because the topography of Schoharie County is very much like the lands in Germany along the Rhine River. At that time, Schoharie was the poorest county of New York State. Yet that was where Fay and I decided—rather, that was where our *bank* decided—we were going to put down our roots.

The farm we found dated back to 1802. There were no nails; it was all just tongue and groove, and wooden pegs. They even had a cistern in the basement where they caught water to bathe and wash their clothes with. There were hand pumps out on the lawn and a door leading to the outhouse. Even though there was indoor plumbing and the house had been updated by its previous owner, the telltale signs of how old the place really was became evident as we walked through. The house had a summer kitchen, a winter kitchen, and a wood-burning cooking stove. Yet all in all, as I told Fay, the place was quaint.

The time came to make the decision to buy or pass. I asked the real estate broker for an hour or two to think about it. Fay and I drove to a McDonald's, and over a cup of coffee and danish I asked her what she thought. She looked me straight in the eye. "I think you're crazy," she said, "but you know, Warren, that never stopped you from doing anything before. Whatever you decide to do, I am behind you one hundred percent." With that, we went back to the real estate office, and the farm in upstate New York became ours. We still had our house in Oceanside, and I had not yet closed the kennel, but I finally had a place to bring the animals.

Back on Long Island, the landlord of Pet Resorts International gave us one to two weeks to vacate the kennel. Beside letting our boarding clientele know that we were not accepting any more reservations, how would I remove all my equipment? There were a hundred plus dog runs, not to mention the two twelve-hundred-pound pigs, chickens, ducks, and geese. How would I transport everything up to the farm in just a weekend? I didn't even have a lot of time to take off. I asked Deco, my best friend, to help me out. So, with the assistance of Deco, his son, and one of my trainers, we rented a truck and caravanned upstate. I even rented a horse trailer for the pigs. The dogs, of course, went in the back of my car.

The funniest part of the trek occurred while driving through Garden City. For those of you who do not know Garden City, it is a rather exclusive, conservative section of Long Island; the seat of justice for Nassau County. I recall driving along, towing the trailer with the pigs. All of sudden Deco yells out from the truck behind me, "You're leaking something!"

"What could be leaking," I thought, "there are no fluids in the trailer." The next thing I hear is Deco, breaking up hysterically, and yelling out the window, "The pig is pissing all over Garden City." All I thought was how would I explain this to a cop: "Well, officer, I'm just driving through Garden City with two pigs, six chickens, six ducks, and eight dogs on my way to upstate New York." Luckily, we were never stopped.

The drive to upstate New York was very treacherous. All the trucks had trouble climbing the Adirondack Mountains. And the truck pulling the trailer, swaying and rumbling, threatened to jackknife. It was quite a dilemma because we had to make it, there

Hanging out with one of the draft horses at the Sunshine Fair in Cobleskill, New York.

were no options. We had only one day to set up all the dog runs, and the barn for the ducks, chickens, and rabbits. Nonetheless, we succeeded!!

I kept the farm for nearly ten years. Fay and I visited every weekend religiously. We would do the Saturday radio show, and then drive up. It was our escape route, and our special time to be with the animals. There was nothing like bringing your head and ego back to where they should be by cleaning up the pig house or the hen house, which was my job most of the time.

Over a Sunday breakfast of coffee and freshly laid eggs, we'd contemplate the big news carried in the local newspaper, the *Mountain Eagle*. The front-page stories included "Sign Appears Mysteriously on Schoharie Covered Bridge" and "Preston Hollow Baptist Church Gets a Grant." Weather would be described as "Autumn colors in the making."

Spending time at the farm, I had the chance to meet some incredible people. There was this great family that owned a dairy farm next door to us. Rosie Ward was like a second mother to Fay and me. She and her family had lived in the area for five generations. She had never left New York, or even traveled on an airplane. The Wards were true farmers. They were good honest people, and kept us in great shape by caring for our animals.

In 1985 we were up to six dogs, twenty-two rabbits, six chickens, six ducks, one pig, two birds, one guinea pig, two hamsters, one gerbil, and twenty to twenty-five cats. The "vacancy" sign was always posted!

Some people may wonder how I accumulated my menagerie for the upstate ark, as I called it. You read earlier how I came across the pigs, now let me explain my chickens, my ducks, and my rabbits.

I was doing a segment on the television show "Saturday Morning Live" for Easter. The concept was "Buying ducks or rabbits as Easter gifts is *not* a good idea," because every year people would buy them as gifts, and the innocent animals wound up being let loose to die on the streets or uncared for at the Humane Society. I borrowed six chicks, six ducks, and six rabbits from a pet store. After doing the segment and spending the night with all of them, I knew I had to keep them. They were going to be mine, a fluffy fuzzy big-eared part of the Eckstein clan.

A week after we brought them up to the farm, I got a call from Rosie. "Warren, you're a father."

"What do you mean: I'm a father," I punctuated with a shout.

The rabbits, whom I thought I had separated perfectly as males and females, were not separated as well as I thought. And sure enough I had a litter of rabbits. Two days later, I had another call from Rosie. "Warren, congratulations. You're a father again."

The bottom line was my six rabbits multiplying to twenty-two rabbits, at which point I was finally able to separate those which had to be separated, and had some of them neutered and spayed.

What do you do with twenty-two rabbits? Well, after moving from the kennel on Long Island to the farm upstate, there wasn't a whole lot of cash reserve. So I built these incredibly large runs, like dog runs, and made them rabbit proof, so each of my rabbits had a six-by-ten-foot area, which was really expansive for them.

For the cooler weather, I built the bunnies hutches in the loft of the barn where the hay was warm. And I have to tell you that all of the rabbits, all twenty-two of them, lived to be between five and eight years old, which is pretty good for rabbits.

My six chickens and six ducks were another story. They got along pretty well, but one of the ducks broke its leg, and the chickens and the other ducks became really aggressive toward it. I had to separate this duck from the others while I called around to almost every vet I knew. They all had the same answer: "What can you do, they don't manufacture artificial limbs for ducks."

I took matters into my own hands. I went to the upstate barn and found some metal and some wood. And God bless my father who taught me how to use tools and be very good with my hands, for I was able to make an artificial limb for the duck. It wasn't attractive, but it worked. I removed it after the leg healed and the duck, named Snowflake, was able to walk, though with a limp. Now, what was really fascinating was that the other ducks and chickens wouldn't accept him with his limp, and once again he had to be isolated.

Then I noticed that Snowflake would keep looking at my pig from across the meadow, and my pig Corky kept looking at the duck. I turned to Fay. "Wouldn't it be a great idea if we could put them together and see if they get along?" They were both lonely. So I brought them together and it was love at first oink. They absolutely adored each other. Their entire lives were spent with the duck on the pig's back, picking off flies, and the pig playing with the duck. It was just fascinating to see how gentle the pig was. Corky, a female, was always very careful where she stepped, to make sure she didn't tread on the duck. They were the most adorable pair—the Laurel and Hardy of the animal world—and they were together for about four years, until Corky died at age twelve.

Up at the farm were some twenty stray cats, and they all wisely decided that the gourmet chow at the Eckstein house was a lot better than chasing rats and mice in the neighborhood barns. They started hanging out, and of course I had them spayed and neutered and placed indoors. They pretty much got along and had great meals and slept in the barn. It was just fascinating to watch all my animals in their kingdom.

The true meaning of Hog Heaven! Corky, Snowflake, and me.

At that time, I had eight dogs. I had Phoenix, my Doberman; Larry, the Old English sheepdog; and Tige, the American Staffordshire terrier, the Buster Brown dog; as well as five that had started out as strays.

Shannon was a fascinating dog, one of the dogs I became closest to. I came to own her while I was a peace officer. A woman driving her car in front of me with a young child pulled over to a lot on the side of the road and just threw this eight- or nine-week-old puppy out of the side of the car and took off. I guess it wasn't this woman's day—what with a county of two million people and twelve peace officers, what were the chances of me being behind her that day? I pulled her over and issued her a citation, then took the puppy to a veterinarian who told me, "Warren, there is no way this dog is going to live. She's suffering from distemper and we should put her to sleep." I didn't accept that verdict because earlier I had given her some food and she ate it. (I always keep dog and cat food in my car for emergencies. Some people carry spare tires, I keep animal chow.) So I thought, let's just see how she does overnight.

The next morning the vet called to say, "Warren, she has distemper and it's still touch and go, but she's eating, so what do you want to do?"

In reply, I said, "As long as she's eating and as long as she's not in any pain, let's let her live."

Just days later she was up and doing fine. She had yellowing of the teeth, which is normal with distemper dogs, but Shannon lived to be eleven years old as one of the greatest dogs in the world. I actually taught her to sniff out drugs, and she was a demonstration dog for me.

Another day a dog came trotting down to the kennel, a little wire terrier mix. After watching for about half an hour and realizing she was a stray, I kind of coaxed her in and named her Honey. She was now another of Warren's dogs, the Peter Pan of the dog world. She had incredible energy and *flew*—I never saw this dog with all four feet on the ground at one time. In fact, I used her on the cover of my book *Pet Aerobics*.

Then there was this little old lady. Lady was a dog that someone had brought in to the kennel while they went on vacation, but they never came back, deserting her at eleven years old. She loved everyone but me. Finally, the last year or so that we had her, a special bond developed between the two of us. It likely resulted from my rescuing her from a deadly Conti Mondi (which I tell about in another chapter). After that, Lady only wanted to be around me.

At this point, I also had Shep. He had also been abandoned near the kennel, which was the probable cause of his really bad attitude. He was the sweetest dog in the world; he just liked to come on strong. We took him in at the kennel and tried to adopt him to three different homes. He was returned the first two times because, while he wasn't that big of a dog, he snarled at the owners. The third time was by a young couple who had just gotten married. I will never forget how they called me from a portable phone in their closet, because the dog had chased them in and they were afraid to come out. Could I come over and get them? So I guess that was Shep's "third strike and you're out," because he wound up spending the rest of his life with me.

Lastly, there was Mugs, one of those dogs I found on the streets in New York City. One night I was driving home from a training session, around 11:30, when I saw this stray on the street looking really disheveled and hunchbacked. She wouldn't come when I got out of the car, so I just sat there for about half an hour with her.

I remember calling Fay and saying, "I'm going to be late."

"Why?" she asked. "Are you chasing another stray?"

"You bet I am!" I laughed. Finally, I coaxed her into the car, and Mugs was just one of those shepherd mixes that lived just to be played with, lived to be hugged and kissed. And believe me, she was hugged and kissed!

So that was my array of animals at the kennel, up at the farm, and testing the legal limit in my home on Long Island. In the past six years, one at a time they went on to pet heaven.

But I have to tell you, I believe that when the time comes, I will meet them again. . . . because there could be no heaven without animals and people living together.

All's Fair

WHAT'S MY LINE. THE ADDAMS FAMILY. ON THE WATERFRONT. PIPPIN. "I NEVER PLAYED THE GAME." What do they all have to do with *Memoirs of a Pet Therapist?* One of the organizations for which I serve on the board of directors is the Bide-A-Wee Home. Bide-A-Wee is a Scottish expression meaning "stay a while," and, fittingly, this very worthwhile organization has operated no-kill animal shelters continuously since 1903. One of their shelters is located in Westhampton, which is on the exclusive east end of Long Island. Each summer they would hold a Children's Pet Fair, and I would participate as one of the celebrity judges along with cartoonist Charles Addams; actress Peggy Cass; Howard Cosell; the fighter Gerry Cooney; Budd Schulberg, who wrote *On the Waterfront*; Michel Bouvier (uncle of Jacqueline Kennedy Onassis); and Broadway choreographer Bob Fosse. Other celebrities joined us along the way, but this was the chief lineup.

What a group to be included in! Every year Fay and I would take a ride to Westhampton and literally hundreds of kids would be out there with their dogs and cats, horses, birds, rabbits, guinea pigs, monkeys, and snakes. There was just about every animal out there, and we had different contests for the kids; you know, Longest Tail, Cutest Pet, Pet that Kissed the Best, Most Dressed-Up Pet. One year a prize was actually awarded to "invisible pets"—a magnifying glass was necessary to see the colony of one-and-a-half-day-old sea monkeys! It was a really great time and a fun fair for everyone who went out there. It is one of those events of which I have tremendously fond memories.

On the eve of the fair, the judges were asked to attend a gala cocktail party that served as an annual fund-raiser, usually held at a place where only the rich and famous would be. For instance, one year the location was the Shinnecock Hills Country Club, which is the oldest golf club in North America, established in 1894. At the beginning I was really starstruck, even though a lot of the attendees weren't typical celebrities but rather Fortune 500 types: CEOs, CFOs, and presidents of major U.S. companies like American Express. Talk about feeling like a fish out of water! Every man would be wearing the paisley sports jacket or the uniform white pants and blue jacket. The ladies floated across the

Doing fashion shots with a designer's dog named Joe Nolan. I can always remember the dogs, but never the owners' names!

room in their gowns, with everyone sipping expensive champagne and wine; or drinks like manhattans and Rob Roys. With Fay asking for a glass of Gallo and me requesting a Schlitz beer, we just did not fit in.

However, animals are great equalizers, and because these people were all animal lovers, they were as excited about being around me as I was intimidated being around them! They had a tremendous amount of respect for the work we did with animals, and were fans of mine from the radio show or from watching me on the various television shows that I did.

So it became "same time, next year"—the only time I would see these people. Yet, gradually, I began to feel comfortable. In fact, one day Charles Addams took me for a ride in his Bugatti (an Italian racing car), which was just one of his very large collection that was worth absolutely a fortune.

It was a fascinating time. I had my first exposure to the east end of Long Island. You would think that since I grew up on Long Island I would have spent some time there, but until I judged this show, I don't think I had been that far east. The east end of Long Island was a place where the wealthy people went in the summertime, not the Eckstein clan. Yet, over the years, more and more of my clients moved out there, so one day a week, over the summer, I would be working with clients in towns like Southampton and Quogue and Bridgehampton.

As uncomfortable as these events might have been for me, I admired these people who generously donated their time and energy to raising money to help animals.

Book Tours

Spokesperson tours eventually became book tours.

The first book Fay and I wrote, back in 1979, was for a small publishing house in Loveland, Colorado, and was titled *Yes Dog, That's Right! A Positive Approach to Training*. While the presentation was basically textbook style, the content is something I'm proud of even today. I was reminded of that just recently at an appearance in the San Francisco Bay area. The people in line all had their copies of *How to Get Your Cat to Do What You Want* or *How to Get Your Dog to Do What You Want* for me to sign; then someone stepped forward with a very intact copy of *Yes, Dog* and said, "Warren, you were ahead of your time. All the pet things people talk about today—like Assistance Dogs, the cruelty of prong collars, and the importance of hugs & kisses—were all in your book seventeen years ago! You can't imagine how many friends have borrowed this book over the years to train their pets, and they're the most well-behaved group of dogs you've ever seen!" I have to admit I laughed out loud, looking at the training techniques illustrated in that book. Me with a scruffy beard, long hair, in my "best" army fatigue shirt and sagging-butt jeans (no wonder I had trouble getting past the doormen in Manhattan), and Fay in her granny dress and rolled up blue jeans. But he was right—the message about the efficacy of the Hugs & Kisses method of training your dog was all there.

The second book we cowrote was entitled *Pet Aerobics*, an exercise book for dogs and cats that was published in 1984. Having worked with more than twenty thousand pets by that point, we knew that exercise and diet could cure a million ills. Within our own menagerie, we had a cockatiel that roller-skated and a pig, Corky, that was once a champion skateboarder. I regularly jogged for a mile down the road at the farm in upstate New York with Spotty, our other pig. Pets need exercise as much as people do, but a short walk to the corner twice a day or to and from the litter box just isn't enough. With *Pet Aerobics* we started pets on the road to fitness with exercises like jumping jacks, push-ups and sit-ups, along with hoop jumping, jogging, and disco dancing!

The timing of the book and the title coincided with the fitness rage of the eighties, and we picked up the nickname "the Jane Fondas of pet exercise"! The idea of an exercise book that helped pets

Spotty and me getting ready for our morning jog!

Tige and I doing our trampoline workout. The neighbors locked their doors when I moved in!

and owners get into better shape generated *incredible* coverage. From *USA Today* to a four-page spread in *People* magazine, *Pet Aerobics* caught the attention of thousands of newspapers and magazines across the country, and also resulted in interviews with some foreign press: *Gente* in Italy, London's *Daily Mail*, and *Reise* in Germany.

At that point, everyone was trying to book me for their shows. I did staircase sprints on "The Tonight Show," and showed how to give a kitty massage on "Good Morning America." On "Hour Magazine," Tige and I demonstrated our owner/pet fitness program on the trampoline. I appeared on local cooking shows whipping up recipes from the book, like Spinach Soufflé and, for overweight pets, Pet Food Au Jus. It was a colossal undertaking to find the right pets for all these different television shows. We needed specially trained dogs to demonstrate the exercises in the book, and there were not a lot of pet aerobics classes going on in Altoona or Louisville! Fay spent eighteen hours a day on the phone. The book tour was very physical and grueling, because of the exercise demonstrations and the scores of local interviews we gave, but Fay and I were determined to make the most of every publicity opportunity that came our way that could make *Pet Aerobics* a big seller. There was just one giant snafu: *There were no books in the stores during the three-city tour!* By the time we realized the problem, we were exhausted and devastated. After that experience—and it was repeated in 1987 with our book *Understanding Your Pet*—I swore we'd never write another book.

Several years later, we were contacted by Peter Gethers, who introduced himself as a fan of the radio and television shows and a cat lover. He was also an editor for Villard Books, a division of

Random House, and he wondered if we would be interested in writing a book on cat behavior. Even after a five-year "cooling off" period, I had still sworn off writing any more books, although Fay and I continued to pen hundreds of articles for magazines like *Woman's World*, *Good Housekeeping*, and *Cat Fancy/Dog Fancy*. Peter was persistent, and even after I had told him no a dozen times, he insisted on having lunch the next time I was in Manhattan. We sat down, and with some solid reassurance from Random House, we went on to write *How to Get Your Cat to Do What You Want*.

When *How to Get Your Cat* was released in 1990, I got my first taste of what a real book tour was all about. Interestingly enough, as I stated earlier, most of the time when I toured, whether to publicize a book or as a company spokesperson, I had public relations people accompanying me from city to city. When I did the *Cat* book, however, I encountered for the first time what they call escort services. When the publisher first said, "We'll have an escort waiting for you at your hotel," I quipped, "Hey, you guys supply everything, don't you?"

But seriously, what had happened is, on an extensive twelve-city tour like this one, they found it was less expensive and more productive to have individuals who were really savvy about each city "escort" the authors around. Most of the escorts I worked with were retired; many of them were former teachers, librarians, and people of all interests, but really pleasant, well-educated people who knew their towns well.

Upon hearing about my spokesperson tours and book tours, my friends would say, "Oh, that's so great; you're traveling all over the country." But in reality, all you see is the airport, the hotel room, and dozens of studios. It's very exhausting—exciting, but exhausting. Over the years, the new thing has become the satellite media tour. Rather than send an author to ten, fifteen, or twenty different cities, the publishers and public relations firms set all the interviews up at a single studio. I've done one at the HBO studios in New York, as well as studios in Los Angeles. With the satellite media tour, you're beamed by satellite to all the local markets they can schedule within their own programming, whether it's "Good Morning Dallas," the afternoon news shows, or "A.M. San Diego." It's more flexible, and you can accomplish in just hours what it used to take days of touring around the country to do.

The other aspect that is interesting about the satellite tours is that you can reach a lot more people. I recently did a spokesperson tour for the Merck Corporation, publicizing their Flea and Tick preventative. Twenty-five or twenty-six different interviews all over the country were arranged for me to complete in about four hours: everything from CNN to Richmond, Virginia, to Bakersfield, California, to Boone, Iowa. It's all very high tech, and consequently you don't have to travel as much. It takes some of the romance out of the job, but it's less complicated.

It was also these tours that gave me the opportunity to meet a lot of different people. People like radio host Kevin McCarthy in Dallas, Texas, who is a good friend of mine; Warren Pierce in Detroit, another radio host; and air personalities like them around the country who are really powerful in their markets. By traveling and meeting these people on more than one occasion, we'd establish a good rapport while joking about dogs and cats—as happened when I first went on the air for Kevin McCarthy's show to promote *How to Get Your Cat to Do What You Want.* He was one of these people who said "Cats are stupid. Cats are dumb, why would anyone want to be bothered having a cat." He was a dog man.

As the years went by and we would do interviews every few months, he started softening. It took me a year or so, but now I believe he owns two cats and says, "How can people own dogs? Cats are better pets, aren't they?" So these media tours can establish good friendships that last a lifetime, and looking back, they were exciting experiences. Still, I'm glad I was younger when I did them; I don't know if I'd survive doing one now!

The Birth of "The Pet Show"

Are you being hustled by your Himalayan? Is your dachshund acting demonic? Does your cockatiel have you crazed? If you love animals, care about wildlife and the environment, and want to really get into your pet's head, stay tuned, because once again, it's time for "The Pet Show," America's only call-in pet psychology show! Hello everyone, I'm Warren Eckstein and this is "The Pet Show." Join the ever-growing Pet Show family. Coming up on today's show:

• Do you bribe your pet? Do you make your dog sing the "Star Spangled Banner" for a biscuit?! Why food rewards are not a good idea!
• Flatulent Fido banned from major TV sitcom!
• Look at your pets right now. Are they depressed? Would you know if they were? Recognizing pet depression.

From "Hour Magazine," many other things started to happen for me. In New York, I became known as "The Pet Authority,"

"The First Pet Shrink," and "The Father of Pet Psychology." People would identify me by all these incredible labels, which led to curious radio stations across the country calling for interviews. I'd always try to get the information across in a funny, entertaining way as well as answer questions from the listeners.

I discovered that pet owners have a different language! Their pets don't pee and poop, they "rainy rain," whiz, leak, piddle, or "do their business" (which always causes me to ask "Tell me, is your pet a lawyer or a CPA?"). Instead of learning how to housebreak their dog or cat, they want to potty train Fido or Fluffy. When the animals poop in the house, callers claim they "left a present" (talk about someone easy to please!). They also say their pets leave behind "cigars," "Tootsie Rolls," "little steamers," "poopsies," and "Baby Ruths"! While poking (mild) fun at their dilemmas, my message would usually be: Treat animals with kindness and affection and most behavioral problems can be overcome. In 1986 I did almost eighty radio interviews in the United States, Canada, and even Italy. Then I started getting requests to be on the most prestigious radio stations, like WOR Radio in New York. A talk-show host named Joan Hamburg (who is still on the air at WOR) called me to do a segment on kids and pets. Of course, I said "sure," and when I went on, the phones rang off the hook. I sat in on the show a second time and again it was a great success. When Joan went on vacation for a week, program director Bob Bruno asked me if I would sit in for Joan one day. "I'd love to," I answered. Although I was nervous, I was doing what I normally do: answering questions about pets and trying to build better relationships between the animals and their owners.

This guest hosting continued, and I would fill in for Joan or other hosts who might have been on vacation. WOR was the number one radio station in New York at the time; consequently, I was ecstatic when they expressed how pleased they were with my work and that they would love to start a regular show with me! But, they added, "On WOR, there is no bad real estate." These media terms always amaze me: They meant that all the shows had good ratings so there was no space to fit me in.

About a year later, the doctor who hosted the medical show on WOR had a disagreement with management and left the station. During that time, I filled in on Saturday afternoon for a few weeks while they searched for a permanent replacement. In the meantime, Bob Bruno called me. "Warren, I'd like you to meet me for lunch at the '21 Club.'" The "21 Club," hmmm—that meant I had to put on a tie and jacket.

This was the time when WOR was owned by RKO, and entertaining lavishly on expense accounts was the eighties thing to do. Well, I recall the meeting well. The same day this meeting was to take place, Fay and I were busy in the morning with Colgate Palmolive on some new pet lines, and I couldn't remember if I was supposed to meet Bob at the "21 Club" or at the station. So I first went to the station, only to find out that Bob had already left. I had to run so as not to be late. I was so anxious to get there on time, I was breaking a sweat.

In any case, I made it safely to the restaurant. We settled in and got to talking, whereupon Bob casually asked me if I wanted my own show. "Are you kidding?" I salivated. And so it was ten years ago that I started on WOR. Early on, I learned the three R's of radio: ratings, revenue, and renewal, which translated to ratings are important, revenue (sales) for the show is even more important, and if you do both well, your show will be renewed! Ironically, the sales department at WOR didn't think a pet show would make it and, more to the point, didn't think they'd *ever* find advertisers. So, it was on *my* shoulders to create sponsorship of "The Pet Show" within the pet industry. While advertisers were obviously vital, the station supported me in my request to have prior approval of any sponsor being approached for my show. When it comes to a product, I wanted my audience to know that I will only endorse it because I would use it on my own pets, not because the show needs underwriting. At that point, my twenty years of credibility were on the line, and I wouldn't consider endorsing a product just to collect a paycheck.

The pet industry tends to be controlled by a "good old boy" network, which frowned at my stand against the "crating" (which is really a fancy word for caging) of animals, as well as the use of prong collars for dogs. I wasn't endearing myself to the veterinary community either, with my position on declawing (which ought to be illegal, like it is in England). Fortunately, the show attracted some visionary young entrepreneurs whose businesses have grown along with me during my years on WOR. One of them (who ultimately became a close friend) is Neil Padron, who had started with a chain of forty pet stores in the New York area, called Petland Discounts. Today, Petland Discounts is the largest independently owned chain in the United States, with 110 stores in New York, New Jersey, and Connecticut!

Then a fellow named Joe Weiss called me from California. He

claimed to have a new product that "would appeal to 100 percent of the 'Pet Show' audience." The more he tried to get it on the store shelves and compete with the "old boy network," the more doors were slammed in his face. Finally, an East Coast friend suggested to Joe that he contact me and see if I would put my seal of approval on it. I was skeptical about the appeal to 100 percent of pet owners until I tried it. His product was an odor neutralizer called Nature's Miracle, and for sure, what pet lover among us hasn't needed to clean up our little angels' accidents? *And* discourage them from returning to the scene of the crime? From the moment Nature's Miracle started on "The Pet Show," Joe not only pushed his product into the stores, but expanded his business into an entire line of pet products. There was only one problem: He couldn't hear the show in Los Angeles! Armed with his enthusiasm, he contacted George Green, the president/general manager of legendary KABC, the leading talk radio station in Los Angeles. KABC had a weekend lineup of "magazine type" shows already in place: a cooking show, a show that featured restaurant reviews, and a travel program. George was open to the idea of adding "The Pet Show" provided he liked what he heard. And this is an example of what he heard:

WARREN: Welcome to "The Pet Show."

CALLER: Good morning.

WARREN: How are you doing today?

CALLER: Well, I'm fine, and you?

WARREN: I'm doing absolutely super.

CALLER: Well good, I seem to have a problem.

WARREN: I hope it's your pet that has the problem.

CALLER: Well, we can't be sure, my husband thinks the answer to this problem is to get rid of *me*.

WARREN: Well, that ought to tell you something, you're skating on thin ice right there already.

CALLER: I know. I have two cats, Butch and Spike . . .

WARREN: Butch and Spike.

CALLER: We've had them seven or eight years. My husband loves Butch very much and Butch is very attached to my husband, follows him everywhere, sits with him, lays on him. Everything. The problem I have with Butch is that he pees on the bed, but he only pees on *my side* of the bed.

WARREN: So, switch sides with your husband. I guarantee you, if you switch sides with your husband the cat will pee on that side of the bed. You know why the cat's doing it?

CALLER: Why?

WARREN: You told *me*. The cat is really attached to your husband.

CALLER: Yeah.

WARREN: You're like the other woman.

CALLER: Well, he doesn't do it all the time and I've tried to figure out what causes this, but out of nowhere he will just go.

WARREN: Out of nowhere from *our point of view*. It may be out of *somewhere* from the *cat's point of view*. Number one, the cat's in good health, I'm assuming?

CALLER: Perfect health.

WARREN: OK. What you need to do is: Get your husband out of the picture. You need more bonding time with Butch.

CALLER: So, what? My husband can sleep in the other room?

WARREN: Your choice. The more time you spend with Butch, and the more bonding you do with Butch, the more you'll become part of Butch's inner circle. Right now he's peeing on your side of the bed to let you know that he is with your husband, and he's letting you know that he's in charge there. So two things: spend more time on the bed with Butch, number one; number two is, whenever you leave the house, for the next couple of weeks, put some of Butch's dry kibble on a paper plate and leave that on your side of the bed.

CALLER: Actually, when we're not here and even if we're home and we're downstairs, I just close the door.

WARREN: Yeah, but that's not resolving the problem.

CALLER: I know that.

WARREN: We want to resolve it. So what I want you to do is I want you to take some of Butch's favorite food, put it on your side of the bed where he's peeing. Tell your husband, it could be worse, he could be peeing on his side of the bed, you know. Also, I want you to use some Nature's Miracle to make sure you get rid of any odor that may have seeped into the mattress, that's important as well, and I think your're going to be on target. But, all joking aside, psychologically I've put Butch on the couch, I've analyzed the problem, I know exactly what's causing it, you need to spend more time on your side of the bed with Butch.

CALLER: I've made a real effort to pet him more, to be more attentive to him, and to cuddle with him.

WARREN: But you've got to get your husband out of the picture.

CALLER: OK.

WARREN: You've got to spend private time.

CALLER: I just need to tell my husband that he can no longer come into the bedroom.

WARREN: Exactly. Your husband is banished from the bedroom. That's it. Another problem resolved here on "The Pet Show." We should have divorce lawyers advertising on this show!

CALLER: I don't set the alarm here on a Saturday morning at seven o'clock for just anything.

WARREN: But you set it for me?

CALLER: I did.

WARREN: All right, my kind of person. Hey, let me ask you a question. How would your pets describe you as an owner: excellent, good, or needs a little work?

CALLER: Butch is in question, but I think we're very good pet owners.

WARREN: Obviously you care about them, and you get up early on a Saturday morning to listen to my show.

CALLER: I love them dearly.

WARREN: Anyway, give them a hug and a kiss for me.

CALLER: OK, thank you.

WARREN: Bye now.

I don't know if George is passionate about animals, but he must have liked the tape, because "The Pet Show" has been on KABC since 1989. The show obviously has tremendous loyalty in listenership so advertisers strongly support it, and we just have a good time. Why? Because I don't take myself seriously on this show. I talk about and give out some of the most incredible information, behaviorally; the audience comes to me for tips they can't get anywhere else. We always joke that veterinarian shows very often fail because when I put a vet on the air with me he or she is interesting for only a couple of minutes; shortly after, we lose the audience's attention. The reason for that, in most cases, is because when you ask a medical question about your pet, you'll be told to take him to your vet so he or she can see it. Whereas if your cat is peeing on the floor, or your dog is having sexual relations with your neighbor's kid . . . this is what my show is about. The biggest frustrations in the world are dogs that have behavioral problems or birds that are screaming in the middle of the night, and these are the reasons people get rid of their pets.

The show's success is based on the fact that it's a very interactive format; we have a lot of fun because my *audience* is the show, and they are delighted to hear solutions to the everyday problems they face living with their four-legged best friends! Besides the phone lines being constantly busy, I knew the program was impacting pet owners by the sacks of mail coming into both WOR and KABC every week:

Cynthia from Cos Cob, Connecticut: "Dear Warren, Brunhilde, my German shepherd, and I understand each other much better since I've been listening to you and following your advice! You have a great program benefiting so many of us pet owners."

Lila from Neptune, New Jersey: ". . . Thank you for the information you provided on how to improve the relationship between my two cats, Sarah and Gaby. I can't believe the difference it made! Two cats that could not be in the same room are at this moment sitting on either side of me on the bed."

Susan in Long Beach, California: "Thanks to you, I get more joy from my two cats than I did before I found you. I have always admired your kindhearted approach to solving pet problems. Thank you for educating people how to treat their pets with kindness."

Yvonne in Morristown, New Jersey: "I, like you, have communicative ability with animals, so needless to say, I really appreciate listening to your show."

And from Van Nuys, California, Rosemarie: "We especially enjoy your question of the week. You once had a question like, 'Do you talk differently to your pets?' When Frank and I first got married, he couldn't tell if I was talking to him or the cats. Everyone in the house is called 'Sweetheart' and 'Baby.' "

The Question of the Day became my trademark on the show. Every week, I answer the questions of my radio audience. In turn, I ask my listeners my own question. Here's how some of my fellow pet lovers have responded to the following questions:

Would you leave your spouse if he or she forced you to give up your pet? (95 percent said "yes!")

Do you sing silly songs to your pets? (85 percent admitted that they do!)

Would you give up your pets for a million dollars cash? (99 percent responded "No way!")

Do you tell secrets to your pets? (80 percent 'fessed up to whispering their secrets)

Would you be more concerned if your spouse or your pet was missing? (100 percent agreed they'd be more concerned if their pet was missing)

But on "The Pet Show," I don't just ask the "safe" questions, like in this Question of the Day with a caller.

WARREN: Christina, has your dog ever embarrassed you?

CALLER: Yes.

WARREN: What did he do?

CALLER: When we had company here one time, he decided to bathe himself right in front of us. He did the whole spread thing, but it was even worse because his *little pink pencil* came out—he was having even *more* fun with *it!*

WARREN: I guess that would embarrass you; it would embarrass me! Thank you, bye-bye. There goes my show...

Well, fortunately, it *wasn't* the end. In fact, in 1993, Buckley Broadcasting (the parent company of WOR Radio) came to me with the possibility of syndicating my show. There would be no difference in the format; it just meant that I would be heard in other cities. After a month or two, the affiliate list of radio stations airing "The Pet Show" grew from three/four/five cities until today where we are heard in more than ninety! From Little Rock, Arkansas, to Anchorage, Alaska—and the list expands every week. "The Pet Show" is heard in all top-ten markets across the country, plus the KABC show. Along with the success of the show came the ability to use the power of the microphone to influence an entire nation of pet lovers to unite and help each other in times of need.

During the devastating earthquake in the Santa Cruz, California, area in the fall of 1989, hundreds of terrified cats and dogs were wrenched from their owners; animals were injured and stranded in pet stores destroyed by the quake and stray livestock roamed the streets. In the aftermath, the overwhelming responsibility for these thousands of animals left homeless countywide fell on the shoulders of the Santa Cruz SPCA. When I heard of the plight of these incredible volunteers, I went on the air with a plea for donations to help them and the animals in distress. From the East Coast to the West Coast, hundreds of donations for $10 to $25 flooded into the shelter, and the notes attached with each check were unbelievably touching—they boosted the morale of everyone at the SPCA.

Similarly, in 1994, when the flooding in southeast Missouri wreaked havoc in the Midwest, once more I appealed to my "Pet Show" family to provide disaster relief for this stricken area. In August, this note arrived for my audience from Nancy Richards, administrator for the Humane Society of Southeast Missouri, headquartered in Cape Girardeau, Missouri:

Once again, finding homes for homeless pets on NBC-TV.

Warren,

I just wanted to say a big "Thank You" for the opportunity to be on your show. As you said, New Yorkers have big hearts and so do people from Pennsylvania, Connecticut, and New Jersey. Your listeners are wonderful and have donated thousands so far this week! I cannot express in words how much this has meant to our shelter, and be assured this money will be put to good use. Thanks again to you, your stations, and to all those wonderful, caring animal lovers.

On an entertainment level, we found that even the advertisers joined in the fun! "The Pet Show" has a roster of advertisers who buy time exclusively on my show. That means their advertising message is focused 100 percent on the pet owner; now, there is a department in every radio station that reviews and has to approve the commercials before they go on the air. In some cases, it's known as the traffic department; others call it broadcast standards. Over the years, I have had these departments calling me in near tears, from laughter! No sir, folks, you won't hear "Pee Pee Pads" for housebreaking your dog running on Rush Limbaugh's show.

And how would you like to be the one to read this: "Warren Eckstein here with some great news. As you know, when you walk your dog the law requires you to pick up your dog's poop. Not very pleasant—that is, up till now. Now you simply scoop the poop into a disposable, plastic Scoop . . ."

Or, "There's no bones about it. When you enroll your pooch in the Bone-of-the-Month Club, a box of customized bone treats will arrive on five designated 'dog days,' including April 15, tax day, when 'Every Dog Has Its Day'!"

And how do I do *this* with a straight face? "Does your dog have *bad body odor*? I mean, does he really *stink*? Then it's time to buy Nature's Miracle's Dander Remover and Body Deodorizer."

You know, sometimes when you do radio and television and write for a living, people put you in somewhat of an omnipotent position, and that just doesn't suit me. I've struggled my whole life with this blue-collar versus white-collar conflict, and while my career is primarily white collar now, I would still rather spend my days on my hands and knees playing with the rats, the snakes, the dogs, and the cats. So getting out and talking with the people about their pets and going "hands on" with their animals will always keep me going. One of the stability factors in my life was when I had the farm in upstate New York, because when my ego got too big or when I got too white collar, I would just hop in with the pig dung and start shoveling it around. It's amazing how pig dung can bring you right back to reality. So it's important to me to consistently *be with* the people who listen to my show. There's no separation, like "I'm the host, you're the listeners." It's equality: We do the show together, it only works because you're there. And I hope people feel that way when they listen.

I have a lot of respect for the people I work with, particularly Bob Bruno, Joe Bilotta, and Rick Buckley of the Buckley Broadcasting Group, who have always treated me fairly. "The Pet Show" has been very successful for them, yet ten years ago when they turned those two hours a week over to me, they had no idea how it would be received. But more important than being the first one to speak out about animal behavior on the radio, I was the first one to go out on a limb and say, "It's OK to give emotions and human feelings to your pets; it's the right thing to do." And the audience appreciated that.

Animal lovers are universal, and before long, I hope to be heard across Canada ("The Pet Show" is already heard on CFUN in Vancouver, B.C.) and maybe even Europe. Spread the word!

MORE PERSONAL STUFF

Fay's Story

Sometimes it feels like you and me against the world, and for all the times we've cried I always felt the odds were on our side. And when one of us is gone and one is left to carry on, well then remembering will have to do. Our memories alone will get us through. Think about the days of you and me . . .

The year was 1989 and the month was November. It is a month that I will never forget, because it was one of the most devastating times of my life. Being a diabetic, Fay was quite conscientious about having regular checkups. She had a mole on her belly that she never paid much attention to, but assumed that at her next appointment she would point it out to her doctor and he would say that there was nothing to worry about. Well, the holiday party season had begun and we were at a friend's house. Fay had worn this wide belt, and when we got home, while she was undressing, she noticed the mole was bleeding. So she decided to move up her next doctor's appointment just to be sure. We went to the doctor who was her diabetic specialist; he gave her a physical examination and she showed him the mole. The doctor said that it was most likely nothing to worry about, but she should have it checked by the dermatologist and have him do a biopsy and remove it at that point. This we did, and they even did an extra-wide incision a little to the right and a little to the left, which was a common practice to ensure that no tissue was missed in the analysis.

We went home confident because the doctor never gave us any indication that there was a problem. In fact, he said that it was a 99 percent chance it would come back benign. Well, you can imagine our shock when the doctor called and said the biopsy showed that the mole was a malignant melanoma. Melanoma ... melanoma, what's a melanoma? When you first hear it you have no idea what you're dealing with or how serious it might ultimately be. We went back to the doctor, and he said that 90 percent of the time, when the melanoma has been taken care of early on, there's nothing to worry about. Again we followed the doctor's advice, yet Fay wanted several opinions. Consequently, we went to Long Island Jewish Hospital and the esteemed Sloan-Kettering;

then we saw a specialist in Westchester County who was performing research on making a vaccine out of a person's own melanoma and then injecting it back into the body.

After the melanoma was removed, we consulted with an oncologist who told us it was necessary to look a little further. Another exam showed a lump under one of Fay's arms, and a biopsy determined it was malignant. Obviously, we were concerned about that. Then another lump was found under her other arm, and that was biopsied, too. Fortunately, it turned out to be benign. "Thank God," I thought. I remember walking out of Mercy Hospital on Long Island clapping my hands, saying, "All right! It's not spreading, it's stopped." But it hadn't stopped. A few weeks later, Fay was complaining of stomach pain, and we called her doctor. He sent us to a gastroenterologist on staff at Mercy Hospital. I remember hearing the words that her liver was distended and they would need to admit her to the hospital that night. Walking down the hallway, her doctor told me, "Two weeks, three weeks at the most."

"Well," I absorbed, "two weeks in the hospital; then I'll hire a nurse for her treatment at home?"

The question hung in the air like a twelve-ton weight before he replied, "No. Two weeks is about how long Fay has to live." I was absolutely devastated.

We had never kept any secrets from each other, so we discussed, or tried to, what we were going to do at that point. Neither one of us believed what this doctor had just thrown at us, and we sought out the specialist in Westchester County. He had a more hopeful outlook. As a result, we would commute out to Westchester three times a week for an incredible vaccination that was going to help her. Throughout these treatments, I watched helplessly as she became very ill. I took her over to the emergency room at Mercy Hospital, and the doctor came out of the room to tell Fay's mother, sister, and me that they were going to start a morphine drip. This to me meant it was the end. Her mother and sister were obviously concerned about her and ready to say yes, but they were not in touch with the more optimistic prognosis held by her other doctor. At that point we had a little argument. "I want Fay to have every opportunity to live, and that means putting her in the hands of the doctor in Westchester, because we have more confidence in him," I asserted. They opposed my plan, but I eased my frail wife into the back of an ambulance in order to make the trek from Long Island to Westchester. I was concerned the ambulance might get lost, and since every moment counted, I drove by myself to lead the way. This trip was agonizing and the longest two hours of my life, because, with the ambulance behind me, I did not know if Fay would be dead or alive when we arrived at the hospital. Much to my surprise, she came out of the ambulance in a wheelchair more alert, and she seemed to feel better.

We checked into the Westchester hospital, where she underwent some tests, and slowly, Fay became well enough to go home. We had succeeded in buying her precious time! Remember, she was diagnosed in November and the emergency room doctor predicted she would only last past the first of the year, and now it was May. My wife was a trooper. There's no doubt about it.

She suffered a setback and again we took her back up to Westchester. She continued to fight for her life. When she checked into the hospital, I took a room at the Holiday Inn. We got Fay a private room and I spent twenty-four hours a day with her. The nurses were really good about letting me stay, but I didn't like what I was seeing. Because of her diabetes, she needed constant attention. Consequently, I had the doctor authorize the nurses to give me the syringes so I could administer her insulin on a regular basis. This made me feel more confident. Yet as I sat by the side of the bed, holding her hand, I realized she was slipping away, so I repeatedly told her, "I love you."

She was very incoherent; there weren't any lengthy conversations, but she struggled to deliver these loving words: "You need to find someone because you can't take care of yourself. I love you." Repeatedly, she whispered, "Thank you, Warren, thank you."

And I answered, "Fay, what is it you're thanking me for? If the shoe were on the other foot, you would be doing exactly the same thing I'm doing. It's just the way it is." At this point I didn't believe she was going to go. On May 19, I decided to return home briefly. My mom was coming up to the hospital on a regular basis, and my neighbors were taking care of our dog and cat, but something triggered me on that day to go back to Long Island to get a change of clothes and check on our pets, then come right back to the hospital. I left the hospital and for the two-hour drive back to Long Island I had to fight to keep my eyes open. I checked on Tige and Mowdy—they missed their mom but were doing fine. I jumped into a shower and just laid down in the bedroom to take a five-minute nap before I drove back to the hospital. Just as my eyes closed the phone rang and the nurse's voice stated, "It's over."

Dazed, I said, "What's over?"

"Fay has expired." I was destroyed.

I really think I was in shock as I went about making the funeral arrangements. Fay was one of those people who was never sick a day in her life. When you think of malignant melanoma, you think of people who spend a lot of time in the sun, but Fay was not a sun worshiper. It was just one of those things that happened, and there was no time to prepare for losing her. I suffered a triple loss, any one of which would be devastating: my beloved wife of nearly twenty years, my closest friend, and my business partner.

We would have celebrated our twentieth wedding anniversary in August. She was married at eighteen and died at thirty-six, so more than half of Fay's life had been spent with me. I was the Dreamer; she was the Weaver of my Dreams.

My cat Mowdy, now in kitty heaven, waiting again for the playtime we once had.

When she didn't come home, our animals became very depressed. After Fay died, the three of us—Mowdy, Tige, and me—were sitting on the bed. I was obviously doing a lot of crying at that point, and there were tears in their eyes, too, as I explained to them that their mom wasn't coming home. I promised that I was going to try to do the best I could by them. For those skeptics out there who think it sounds eccentric, let me tell you something: These guys knew exactly what I was talking about and exactly what I needed to do. It was their grieving and my concern for them that eventually pulled me through my personal devastation.

Everyone was advising me to sell the house and move, that I can't dwell in the past, and lots of other well-meaning clichés. But Fay was that house, and my life was that house, so it was not as easy as people thought. And while trying to keep this house together, I still had the farm upstate with all the animals to attend to.

> *"We are each of us angels with only one wing.*
> *And we can only fly embracing each other."*

Would I ever fly again?

The Broken Wing Begins to Heal

After Fay's death, the needle on my emotional compass was spinning wildly; I really felt that my career was basically going to be over. The grief was debilitating and endless; it was a constant struggle not to surrender to the depression that consumed me. I was just going through the motions; I really didn't care much about what was going on. The things that kind of saved me were the commitments that Fay and I had made prior to her death.

One of these was the release of *How to Get Your Cat to Do What You Want*. In fact, I did the audio book while Fay was in the hospital, having to leave and run into a studio in New York to dictate it. Now, just six weeks later, I was supposed to go out on a ten-city book tour. People were telling me not to go, but I thought it was the right thing to do, and so off I went from Seattle to Atlanta to Boston. The days were great and went really fast, because I was so busy and involved with publicizing the book; but the nights tormented me. In cities where I knew absolutely nobody I was alone with my grief, so I would spend a lot of time in the hotel's bar.

In terms of the radio shows, I was actually back on the air two weeks later, and I never mentioned to any of the listeners what happened to Fay—I'm very private that way.

Basically, I kept my mind focused by following up on my commitments. I would see a client now and then to pay a bill, but I wasn't really pursuing that end of it. I was maintaining the financial side of things by doing the radio shows and my appearances on "Live! With Regis & Kathie Lee." While it kept me occupied, I wasn't attempting anything new, and it seemed that my career had reached its pinnacle. I was at the point where I said to myself, "You know what, I'll get a job at the local pet store and just work."

Then one day I got a phone call that, unbeknownst to me, would change my entire life. The voice on the other end of the phone said, "Hello, Warren, my name is Howard West. I'm calling you from Los Angeles and I'm with Shapiro/West. We're a talent management group on the West Coast. You know, I listen to your show every Saturday on KABC Radio and I'm not even a big animal lover. As a matter of fact, I don't even know if I like animals, but you make me laugh! When are you coming to California? I'd like to sit and talk with you."

Quite honestly, at that point I was not pursuing a career in the media, but he sounded like a nice guy, so I said, "Let me get back to you." I called my friend Steve Clements and said, "I got a call from a guy named Howard West, who works for a group called Shapiro/West. He wants to meet with me."

"Howard West and George Shapiro, his partner, are the executive producers of the *Seinfeld* show!" Steve told me excitedly. "Howard has represented Jerry Seinfeld his entire career. He and George Shapiro are very well known and respected managers on the West Coast. Yes, you should *definitely* meet with him!"

I returned Howard West's call and we spoke a little bit more and decided that the next time I was in Los Angeles we would meet. Within a month we were face-to-face at an Italian restaurant, having a good conversation. I must admit I didn't know what to expect. I never had personal management, agents, or anyone represent me in the past. Any contracts that I signed were read over by Fay. So some of the contracts that I've signed in the past were unbelievable and clearly not in my best interests. I wish I had someone representing me years ago; it would have made life a lot easier and I would have been a lot farther along on my career path.

On the other hand, a lot of careers are ruined by poor or dishonest management, and so I considered myself lucky that someone the caliber of Howard West would be interested in representing me. He's a straightforward kind of guy, and we hit it off well. Despite feeling a little intimidated by him, we decided we would form a relationship. It was strange at first. Howard is a guy who can say "no." Prior to meeting him, the word *no* was not in my vocabulary—I said "yes" to everybody. I was known as an easy touch, so I was constantly doing this fund-raiser, that fund-raiser, or driving two and a half hours to do something for free. Howard pointed out, "Warren, it's okay to be charitable; but you know, charity starts at home."

Gradually, I realized that the things *I* was doing for nothing or for token amounts of money *other people* were getting paid considerably well to do! So it was a great relationship and a lot of things started to happen.

As my manager, he came up with the idea of a pet product line with my name on it. Being that my reputation is based on Hugs &

Howard West! He really wants a Hug & Kiss, but sorry, Howard—no way!

Kisses, I felt that would be a great name for a product line, and decided what our first product was going to be. I'm a close watcher of what's hot in the people market, because it's been my observation that whatever we're into now our pets are going to be into five years down the road. So I went right for the vitamin/mineral/supplement line, knowing that's what everyone's hot on. I felt that it would be a beneficial product, something really important for pets in terms of health that their owners would understand because they were taking their own vitamin/mineral supplements.

There was a product on the market at that time that I had been using for twenty, twenty-five years when I used to show dogs and run the kennel. It was a very successful product, but the general public knew nothing about it. It was available (more or less) only to people who were professionals, and they all loved it. I decided to look at that product, make some improvements, and bring it out under the Hugs & Kisses label, calling it: Warren Eckstein's Hugs & Kisses Vitamin/Mineral Supplement. We were going to produce one for dogs and one for cats.

One irrefutable part of my personality, and I guess that's the reason why I'm so successful working with animals, is that I'm an instant gratification type of person. I like to see the results immediately. I hate waiting on line—not that anyone loves it—and I will avoid it at all costs. The same with waiting for a reply. No way! I want an answer right then and there. And that made it difficult, because creating a product line takes considerable time and a lot of thought. By contrast, Howard is one of those rare, visionary people who methodically takes something from A and develops it to Z—I guess that's what a producer does. So he helped guide me along. The Hugs & Kisses product is doing well, so that was our first step. Now we're in the process of coming out with other products that, hopefully, will make Hugs & Kisses a major player in the pet industry.

We also decided to publish a national newsletter, both Howard and I being newsletter fanatics. It's also called "Hugs & Kisses"—the only publication about animals that discusses physiological as well as psychological issues. It's interactive with pet owners, who participate by sending in stories, pictures, and more. Chihuahua Chili, for example, is a recipe that we published in the newsletter, and there's always the "Eckstein" comic. Overall, it's a great forum where pet lovers can feel normal, because sometimes we feel a little crazy in this world when other people say "You do *what* for your cat?"

The relationship between me and Howard has been very strong, and I love working with him. I believe it was kismet that led me to him at that time in my life, when I felt my best professional days were behind me. He's helped me emerge from my personal problems and move ahead with life.

On reflection, nothing's really stopped since Fay died. Yet during those truly bleak days I probably would have left had it not been for Tige and Mowdy and all the animals at the farm. Those commitments kept me going just long enough for me to regain my sanity and restore some direction to my life.

Once again, at a critical moment, I focused on what I love most—the animals—and they brought me back.

Getting Hammered

Since I decided to disregard the advice people gave me to sell the house and move, I had to make changes quickly. Leaving things the same was just too bittersweet, and besides, keeping busy would become my way to deal with losing Fay. At the time, my close friend Deco was out of work, and by profession, he was a carpenter, builder, and contractor. (We had been friends for twenty years and the only time I ever saw him cry was when Fay passed away.)

I didn't want to allow myself too much time to grieve, so instead Deco and I each grabbed a sledgehammer from my garage and started knocking the house down. Outside walls, inside walls—we literally ripped the entire house apart and redid it from top to bottom. For the next six months, we rewired the electricity, installed new plumbing, and insulated and sided the house. I was just totally wiped out of money at this point, with maybe two thousand dollars in the bank, so completing each project depended on the U.S. Mail. I would go to my post office box twice a day to see whether a book royalty check came in, or maybe a residual payment from the "New Mickey Mouse Club." If one arrived, Deco and I would run to the lumberyards. "Hey, let's get six pieces of lumber today, or should we buy a new window?" Or "This was a big score, let's get a sliding door for the back!" Changing seasons would find the two of us shivering in the frigid winter wind, making countertops, and putting on a new roof. It was really an incredible learning experience for me, but it was also my therapy.

After four or five months had passed, Deco kept asking me, "When are you going to start going out; you know, seeing people?"

"No," I said, shaking my head. "I'm taking a vow of celibacy and this is it; I'm going to stay here." But I guess that's how everyone feels when they lose a beloved spouse.

Anyway, one day I was sitting around the house saying to myself, "I just have to get out of here." Now this is going to sound crazy to everyone, but here's how whacked my rationale was: I didn't want to meet anybody; didn't want to talk to anybody. I didn't want to go to a bar where there would be a bunch of people sitting around talking to one another. But in the town next to mine there was the sleaziest topless bar in the world, Bare Necessities. "I think I'll go in there and have a couple of beers and sit by myself," I thought. The chances of meeting anyone in a topless bar are nil; everyone's too involved with drooling over the girls, and the girls are just there to make money. They all have boyfriends, so I felt it was a safe place to go just to get out. The first night I had a couple of beers, then about a week later I went back, and the bartender, Arianna, started talking to me. We became friendly, and so here I was going on my first date in over twenty years, with a topless bartender. I was now entering my self-destructive phase. My mother was no doubt frantic at this point, but using reverse psychology when I revealed Arianna's profession, she casually observed, "Well, it's a living." This tryst went on for a couple of months; I guess I realized she wasn't the girl for me when she showed up at my house, drunkenly waving her arms and slurring, "Look at this shrine you built for your dead wife!" Then one night I was sitting in the bar and a motorcycle gang came in. I knew there was going to be a big hassle here. I looked around and said to myself, "What am I doing here?" I gave up Bare Necessities.

Next I tried going out with a pet industry friend of Fay's and mine who called me when she heard that Fay had died. We went out to dinner, which was awkward. In spite of that, we went on a second date. After taking me to see the movie *Ghost,* she probably guessed she might not be hearing from me again.

Meanwhile, I attended a WOR Radio fund-raiser in my capacity as host of "The Pet Show." I came into contact with a thirtysomething woman who worked at the station in sales. We started talking and she asked me if she could have a ride home. We started going out, and while Deco and I were working at the house one day she called, saying, "I've been laid off, can you help me out?" Hearing how distraught she was, I dropped everything and went into the city. She was obviously depressed, she had lost her job, and I was there to console her. She didn't want to continue living in her mother's one-bedroom apartment, so she started moving her things to my house. We ultimately wound up getting married, another Las Vegas marital success story. Just before we went in to exchange "I do's," two couples (clad in skin and leather) walked out of the Justice of the Peace's office. One of the guys turned to the other and said, "I should have married my Harley." If that wasn't the writing on the wall!

The marriage lasted only two years, but it took me three years of hell to finalize the divorce, which wiped me out financially. A good choice of attorney, I guess.

True Companion

A few years ago, a salesperson from KABC Radio in Los Angeles named Denise Madden called me in New York to bounce some ideas around for a potential advertiser she had for "The Pet Show." It was a pet photography studio where she and her dog had posed for their 1992 holiday card. I just flipped over the beautiful German shepherd in the picture, and Denise told me how she had adopted Rio from Seattle Purebred Dog Rescue and that he'd had four homes by the time he was only eight months old. I came to L.A. a few months later, and he posed with me for some station publicity pictures at the same studio, Pets and People Photography. Rio was even more gorgeous than his picture, but I sensed that he was rather insecure and very timid. He kept walking away during the picture-taking, which really embarrassed his owner, like the dog's supposed to pay me some special respect because I host "The Pet Show." I remember saying, "Denise, it's OK, just let him be a dog!" The photographers, Laura Pavey and Joshua Grenrock, managed to capture a great shot, considering *I* was still in the picture! After that, Denise and I continued to go on sales calls or otherwise got together for the next couple of years whenever I was in Los Angeles.

Our life situations were similar, as she had experienced a painful loss of a family member in 1989, and in her own words, felt the sense of missing pieces in her life. She also described feeling like a very old soul, unable to recapture joy in her life. It was exactly how *I* felt, only I had kept it buried deep inside. I found it comforting to share it for the first time with this near stranger. The other parallel in our lives was how well we both covered up our inner "walking wounded" melancholy. I observed her power to brighten a room and draw people to her. She watched as I cracked jokes nonstop with everyone around me. I realized that our friendship was a stabilizing factor in my life, and what a giant mistake my second marriage had been.

Gradually, as I looked forward to seeing her and Rio once or twice a year, it seemed that I was falling in love with her, and I honestly believe that it was *fate* that brought us together. Such an unlikely pairing with three thousand miles and three time zones separating us. There was a movie once, called *Weird Science*, where two young boys build their ideal woman: physically, psychologically, emotionally, and intellectually. And while I didn't build Denise, that's how I visualized her: as my *Weird Science* project. When I told her how I felt, she was really astounded; we had never taken our brief get-togethers of the last two years to any level beyond that of supportive friend. When she recovered from her surprise, she realized she loved me, too. By letting go of our losses, and permitting ourselves to "fall in love," we began to reconnect the happy bits of ourselves we both thought were lost forever.

We're a perfect balance for each other. I can be moody and Denise is very even-tempered. I happen to be very impulsive. It's not unusual for me to wake up at five or six on a Sunday morning and say to her, "We're going on a road trip today. Let's do this!"

And she laughs and says, "All right, I'm there. Let's go!" She never gets angry, and believe me, I'm an easy person to get angry at! And we have such a good time, we really do. The toughest part

Denise and Rio posing for their holiday card. How could I not fall in love! With Denise, too.

of our relationship has been writing this book, opening up about my life.

Having spent my entire life in New York, other than my military service and some college, I guess I felt it was time to move geographically. A combination of things went into making my decision to move to California. Number one, my manager, Howard West, was there and he is very influential in many of the decisions I make. This move would give me the opportunity to work more closely with him. I also didn't want to be away from Denise, even though she probably would have relocated and moved permanently to New York had I asked her to. She resigned her position as senior account executive at Shamrock Broadcasting and came back to New York with me for six months to help me move my New York–based business to the West Coast. It was an enormous emotional undertaking, starting with the farm.

When Fay died, it was a little more difficult to maintain the farm financially, as well as the physical upkeep. The cost factor of paying my neighbors to take care of the animals and living on Long Island became overwhelming. It was simply too much, and I wasn't getting up there at all. Gradually I realized that the dream of the farm died along with Fay. But I did not have the emotional wherewithal yet to sell it, and I still had the animals. One by one, the animals died of old age after long and happy lives. The average life span of a pig is about eight years, but both Spotty and Corky lived to be twelve. The dogs lived to be fourteen, fifteen years old. Even the chickens far outlived the average life span of chickens. I kept the farm until all the animals had moved on to animal heaven, and then it was time to make the decision. It broke my heart. I tried looking for things that would make me angry at the farm, but the only experiences I recalled were the wonderful times that Fay and I had up there. Finally I accepted the fact that selling the farm was inevitable. I still miss that magical place, but it was the right thing to do. The winter after I decided to sell the farm was one of the worst in New York's history. Between blizzards and wicked snowstorms, I was calling up there and finding out that the entire house was buried by snow. No one could get up to the house to deliver the oil because the snow was so deep! I guess things really do happen for a reason. A young couple bought it, and the legacy of the place will continue, because the new owners were planning to raise a family and some animals there. Knowing that they were going to keep it as a farm made me feel better about selling it. It was built in 1802; hopefully, it will still be around in 2002.

The last day up at the farm was difficult. Denise and I had spent two days packing everything up. How do you close down ten years of a life? I ended up either giving stuff away or throwing it all out. It meant something to me, but I couldn't take it all. I even had my 1970 Duster up there, which I wound up towing back, and I still own it. We rented a U-Haul and towed the Duster and some belongings. With tears in my eyes, I said good-bye to the farm and started the long drive home. I still reminisce about the farm, even though I haven't been back. Maybe sometime in the near future I'll be up in that neighborhood and I'll just kind of drive by and say good-bye under happier circumstances.

▼ ▼ ▼

California is a place I made fun of for many years. It was a running joke, "How could *anyone* live in California?" I'm a New Yorker, everything happens in New York; yet here we were, packing up my Ford Explorer to head west. We had driven Denise's car from Los Angeles to New York; now we had her car *and* my car to bring back to California. We were bringing her clothing back (more than they have on one entire floor at Saks Fifth Avenue!), my clothing (which fit into a plastic bag from the supermarket); a computer, televisions, all of my tax records and business files—everything I had been doing for the last twenty-five years. The entire back of my car was filled, the entire trunk along with the back and front seats of Denise's car (which we were towing) were filled, and some-where, somehow Rio was able to squeeze in. In the back of the car was also a shotgun that I kept in my house for security. So, here we were, packed up and ready to start our three-thousand-mile trek together.

While heading west, I wanted to stop in Nashville, being a big fan of country music, but Denise wanted to see the Osmond Brothers, so I gave in and we spent a few nights in Branson, Mis-souri. Actually, we hooked up there with Denise's parents, Connie and Jim Morse, who lived in Omaha. But before we did, at around 11:30 at night just outside of Branson, Denise nervously said to me, "Warren, pull over; there's a police car behind us with its lights flashing." Now, here's what's going through my head: OK, I have my car with New York license plates, filled to the hilt, with a German shepherd and a shotgun in the back. Denise's car with California plates is also filled to the hilt. I haven't shaved in probably two days and I've been driving for more than twelve hours straight at this point. I looked like I was right off the TV show "America's Most Wanted," so when they stopped us, I said to Denise, "There's a good possibility that there'll be something about me they don't like." Denise, who is totally intimidated by authority figures (from too many years in Catholic school, she explains), would have copped to *anything* regardless of her innocence! Anyway, this state trooper looked my car up and down, inside and out while *his* partner was busy quizzing *my* partner. He decided to write me up a warning because the lights on the trailer I had rented from U-Haul, the "Experts in Moving," were too far forward of the car when I put on the brakes and could not be easily seen. In Missouri, this was against the law. Boy, were we lucky! But it wouldn't be our last encounter with law enforcement on the trip.

We kicked back for a couple of days and had a great time with Denise's parents in Kimberling City, just outside Branson, on the beautiful Lake of the Ozarks, and then it was on to California. Rio, by the way, was just incredible during the entire trip. We stopped every few hours to let him stretch his legs, get a drink of water, and to play with him, but he slept most of the way and just loved it. Every so often, he popped his head up when we'd go by a cattle ranch. I guess the scent in the air woke him up! We did stay in some unusual places, me being the spontaneous type. I told Denise, "We don't have to map things out; let's just get into the car and whenever we get tired, that's where we'll stop." One of our most memorable stops that I don't think she has ever forgiven me for was a place called Shamrock, Texas. There was a motel, and a little restaurant with only one thing on the menu: chicken fried *everything*.

From there we spent the night in Gallup, New Mexico. It was 7:00 A.M. and a hot sun was already rising as I headed out to my truck, suitcase in hand. In the desert brush next to the parking lot of the Holiday Inn, standing stiffly, was a dog looking a little scared and confused. When I approached, it tried to walk away and fell down. I immediately started talking softly and approached slowly. When I got on the ground with the dog, it licked my hand and looked at me with thankful eyes. It turned out that it had a broken hip and was just skin and bones underneath the tar that covered it from being on the run. It was most likely a reservation dog and no one was going to miss it. So, here I am in Gallup, New Mexico, at seven o'clock on a Saturday morning. What do I do with this injured dog? We tried calling the Humane Society but only reached their "after hours" message, and there was no answer at the local vet's. I knew I had to get the dog help. I called the Gallup Police Department and two policemen arrived in a squad car. They were a little fearful of touching the dog because it was hurt, so I picked it up and eased it into the back of the black and white. I felt like I was on the TV show "Cops"—the car door only opened from the outside, and I had a shotgun staring at me from the front seat. They even ran my driver's license through their computer! I pointed out to them, "Hey, guys, do you think I would call the police about an injured dog if I was on the run?" As luck would have it, we found a veterinary hospital willing to help—provided, of course, that I gave them my MasterCard. It turned out that "Gallup," as we so cleverly named the dog, was a five- or six-month-old Australian shepherd with the personality of a saint and so grateful for a real meal. As we headed on to L.A., we called often to see how it was doing. A few weeks later, Gallup came to live with a close friend, Joanne Udell, and they are devoted to each other.

Arriving in Santa Monica, I was really excited but also a little apprehensive and intimidated. People think of New Yorkers as being tough, aggressive, and assertive people, but remember, I was a 516 New Yorker (516 being a Long Island area code). I didn't know

Denise learning that when you fall in love with a pet psychologist, it can really get your goat.

what was ahead for me there. While everyone at "Regis & Kathie Lee," WOR Radio, and WNBC-TV was supportive and worked things out with me so I could continue the shows, I was still insecure. Now that I've been out here almost two years, I don't think there is anything that could make me move back! I love New York, and I have many friends back there, but my home now is definitely southern California. Maybe it's the weather, and the fact that I can be out with the animals all the time. I really enjoy the slower pace, and Santa Monica is a warm, friendly city that feels more like a suburb. I go back to the East Coast every three weeks for the different shows, so I still get my New York fix.

Since I've been in California, many of my dreams have really come true. While Fay was ill, I had promised her that I would realize my dream to create a nonprofit organization to raise money for the thousands of animal rescue groups who do the majority of the work yet are rarely funded. Fay had worked side by side with me all those years and saw the incredible need of these small organizations across the United States who struggle valiantly in their efforts to save animals. Because they don't have the savvy of major p.r. people behind them or a big budget, they're usually running against the wind. The Hugs & Kisses Animal Fund has been granted 501 © (3) status, which I'm really excited about, and by the time you read this, no doubt you'll have heard a lot about the fund and its mission to bestow monetary grants to these "humane heroes" who have demonstrated their compassion for the animal world. To prove we won't take ourselves too seriously with tux and tails fund-raisers, for the last two Christmas seasons I've put on my Santa suit and posed with hundreds of dogs, cats, and even potbellied pigs for holiday cards with the proceeds going to the Hugs & Kisses Animal Fund!

My second dream has always been to own a Harley-Davidson. Denise would do little things to fuel the dream, like buying me one share of H-D stock and gifting me with a pair of H-D boots. And now I have one and I absolutely love it! It's my escape, and it's like being *part* of the environment. Whenever my manager gets on my nerves, which is at least once a day, I just get on my Harley, go for a ride, and let the wind on Pacific Coast Highway blow in my face.

I was not a major figure in my hometown when I was growing up, but as I write these memoirs I remember how amazed I was in 1986 when my hometown honored me in what they called Ocean-side Alive Days. Along with Bob Iger (for whom I now work as the president of ABC, Inc.), major league pitcher Dennis Leonard, and author Joel Gross, I received citations from senators and congressmen as well as the high school I barely graduated from. I was really proud. I had been really uncomfortable with the notoriety I received from my many television and radio appearances. But with Fay's support I came to understand that I had a mission and this was all part of it. In 1989, I was chosen as the recipient of the Genesis Award for Outstanding Radio Talk Show Host. It was an award shared equally in my heart with "The Pet Show" audience for being so receptive to my message of animal welfare.

Growing up, I learned you have to stand for something even if it's unpopular, and over the years many of the positions I have taken on animals have received criticism from the "establishment." My ultimate satisfaction has been to see the establishment hawking the same ideas they criticized me for twenty-five years ago: pets having emotions; pet aerobics, massage, talking to your pets, brushing their teeth—basically treating them like part of the family.

What are my dreams for the future? Well, people say that you should wish for those things that would make you the happiest person in the world. If that's true, then my dreams have already

What's a nice Jewish boy doing in an outfit like this? It must be to raise funds for the Hugs & Kisses Animal Fund, with my friends Kimberley and Kevin Graner.

come true. I'm with a person I love and we plan to grow old together. I live in an area I absolutely adore but with the opportunity to go back and forth across the country frequently. I have the toys I want—my motorcycle, my lawn tractor, my car. What else can a man ask for? I don't need material things like expensive suits and prime real estate. These have never been important to me. As long as I have two pairs of jeans so I can wear one while the other one is being washed, I'm a happy guy.

So in terms of future dreams, I would just like to expand on what is already happening in my life. I have a career that makes people and their pets smile, and the success and notoriety that go

All my dreams come true.

along with it, which I can enjoy. I really believe that what I say on behalf of animals is important. If I can be as successful in the second half of my life as I was in the first, I would consider myself to be complete. Perhaps there will be a second autobiography, but if nothing ever changed and everything stayed exactly the way it is today, I would be a very happy person and I know I'm very lucky to say that.

> Don't be afraid to go out on a limb.
> That's where the fruit is.
>
> —*Anonymous*

Photo Credits

About the Author

WARREN ECKSTEIN has been a pioneer not only in pet psychology but in pet aerobics. He has operated a luxury boarding establishment for pets and has fought, armed, against animal abuse. Many of the animals he has trained have appeared on "Saturday Night Live." After innumerable appearances on "The David Letterman Show," "The Tonight Show," and other network programs, Eckstein now hosts his own nationally syndicated radio show, "The Pet Show." He is also a monthly guest on "Live! with Regis and Kathie Lee" and "NBC Weekend." Among his earlier books is the bestselling *How to Get Your Dog to Do What You Want.* Warren and Denise Madden live in Santa Monica, California.